The Energy Healing Guide for Empaths

Heal Your Highly Sensitive Energy, Set Boundaries, Clear Negativity, and Thrive with Your Supernatural Powers

© Copyright 2025 - All rights reserved.

The content contained within this book may not be reproduced, duplicated, or transmitted without direct written permission from the author or the publisher.

Under no circumstances will any blame or legal responsibility be held against the publisher or author for any damages, reparation, or monetary loss due to the information contained within this book, either directly or indirectly.

Legal Notice:

This book is copyright-protected. It is only for personal use. You cannot amend, distribute, sell, use, quote, or paraphrase any part of the content within this book without the consent of the author or publisher.

Disclaimer Notice:

Please note the information contained within this document is for educational and entertainment purposes only. All effort has been executed to present accurate, up-to-date, reliable, and complete information. No warranties of any kind are declared or implied. Readers acknowledge that the author is not engaging in the rendering of legal, financial, medical, or professional advice. The content within this book has been derived from various sources. Please consult a licensed professional before attempting any techniques outlined in this book.

By reading this document, the reader agrees that under no circumstances is the author responsible for any losses, direct or indirect, that are incurred as a result of the use of the information contained within this document, including, but not limited to, errors, omissions, or inaccuracies.

Your Free Gift
(only available for a limited time)

Thanks for getting this book! If you want to learn more about various spirituality topics, then join Mari Silva's community and get a free guided meditation MP3 for awakening your third eye. This guided meditation mp3 is designed to open and strengthen ones third eye so you can experience a higher state of consciousness. Simply visit the link below the image to get started.

https://spiritualityspot.com/meditation

Or, Scan the QR code!

Table of Contents

INTRODUCTION 1
CHAPTER 1: UNDERSTANDING THE GIFT AND SCIENCE OF EMPATHY 3
CHAPTER 2: EMPATHS VS HIGHLY SENSITIVE PERSONS (HSPS) 19
CHAPTER 3: ENERGY WORK I: ENERGY ANATOMY (CHAKRAS, THE AURA, AND YOUR UNIQUE FREQUENCY) 32
CHAPTER 4: ENERGY WORK II: ENERGY ESSENTIALS AND PRACTICES FOR SENSITIVE SOULS 49
CHAPTER 5: SPIRITUAL DEFENSE I: RECOGNIZE AND RELEASE THE NEGATIVE AND TOXIC 66
CHAPTER 6: SPIRITUAL DEFENSE II: RECOVER FROM NEGATIVE ENERGY DRAINS AND ATTACHMENTS 80
CHAPTER 7: SPIRITUAL HEALING I: ENERGY HEALING TECHNIQUES FOR EMPATHS 95
CHAPTER 8: SPIRITUAL HEALING II: UNBLOCK AND ENHANCE YOUR EMPATHIC ABILITIES 113
CONCLUSION 127
HERE'S ANOTHER BOOK BY MARI SILVA THAT YOU MIGHT LIKE 130
YOUR FREE GIFT (ONLY AVAILABLE FOR A LIMITED TIME) 131
REFERENCES 132
IMAGE SOURCES 145

Introduction

Empathy is one of the greatest personality traits you can have. It turns you into an understanding and compassionate person who people gravitate towards. Sometimes, you can tell how someone is feeling before they even speak. While empathy can make you everyone's favorite person, it can also be quite challenging.

Empaths absorb people's emotions and energies. This makes you sensitive to their negativity and vulnerable to energy vampires and manipulators. However, you can deal with the disadvantages of empathy and high sensitivity with the techniques and tips in the book.

It begins by explaining empathy, its spiritual aspects, and the science behind it to help you understand your energetic nature and why other people's emotions affect you deeply. You will also learn the difference between high sensitivity and empathy.

Empaths often feel drained after socializing for long periods or spending time with toxic individuals. You need to understand how your energy system functions and how to balance it to deal with draining situations.

Energy work practices, such as grounding, breathwork, meditation, and visualization, will ground, clear, and strengthen your energy fields to prevent exhaustion, anxiety, and emotional overload. Incorporating these exercises into your daily routine will help you stay centered and protect you from negative energy.

Your sensitivity to negative energy can impact every aspect of your life. However, many people don't notice when there is a shift in their energy field or when they are in toxic environments. You need to identify and cut cords with toxic people, energy vampires, and draining environments. Meditation, visualization, setting boundaries, and other techniques can help release the negativity you absorbed from these people and places.

You can also practice energy defense and protection strategies to shield yourself from negative energy.

Certain energies, however, can attach themselves to you. To recover from this attachment, you need to recognize signs of energy drain and understand how they are formed.

The last part of the book focuses on spiritual healing. You will learn about powerful healing methods, including Reiki, Qi Gong, breathwork, and visualization techniques that you can use daily.

You will be able to get in touch with your empathic abilities to overcome doubt, fear, past wounds, mental limitations, and physical blockages.

This book offers an accessible approach that is perfect for beginners and provides a pathway to transformation, helping readers shift from feeling overwhelmed to thriving with their intuitive and healing gifts. It is designed specifically for empaths, highly sensitive people, and intuitive individuals, addressing the unique challenges and strengths of those who absorb the emotions and energies of others.

Unlike other energy healing books, this guide provides a step-by-step framework for protecting, balancing, and enhancing your energy field using ancient wisdom and modern techniques. It offers practical, easy-to-apply exercises, meditations, and techniques that help you immediately clear negative energy, set strong boundaries, and strengthen your inner power. It also addresses personal energy healing, spiritual defense, boundary-setting, and developing empathic abilities as a gift, not a burden.

Chapter 1: Understanding the Gift and Science of Empathy

When the mind is allowed to wander a little within the vaults of the memory, sifting through the archives of the past, emotions experienced in certain events may float up to the surface. It can be a friend's wedding, a dinner celebration, or a close acquaintance having a baby. People are often surprised when they remember how they felt. Whether that is happiness for others or feeling as if the joy was, somehow, in part, their own. Some people may feel so deeply for others that it's almost like they're the ones being celebrated. They can feel it so profoundly that it reverberates in their bones.

There's a science behind the workings of empathy.[1]

The same sensations can occur with regretful experiences, like when the brain recalls a bad memory. A classmate received a low grade on a test, or maybe something more serious, at a funeral home when a friend lost someone close. These events can trigger a feeling of discontentment in the people surrounding the person afflicted with the tragedy. Some can simply sympathize and feel sad for the person. Others may feel the need to offer words of comfort to ease their pain.

In some cases, people are so in tune with the emotional state of the afflicted that they may start crying themselves. They can start to picture themselves in their shoes. They feel their sorrow as their own, both physically and emotionally, almost like they themselves lost something or someone.

Is there a difference between these feelings? The answer is yes. As close as they may seem, these emotions and reactions are quite different. Some may qualify as empathy, and some define the person feeling them as an empath. But how can you tell the difference, and what does that mean for you?

As you read on, you'll learn how to identify the emotions you experience, dive deeper into your psyche, and understand how to manage them.

What Is Empathy?

Does having Empathy mean you're an empath by default? Well, that's a loaded question that requires an in-depth answer.

It's suggested that the word empathy is derived from the German word Einfühlung, which translates to "feeling into."

Empathy is a practice in which most, if not all, humans can show and feel at varying levels. That is, unless said human suffers from psychological ailments like sociopathy. It basically means the ability to put yourself in another person's shoes and the capacity to relate to their experiences and appropriately respond to them. That can be by offering caring words, kind gestures, or helpful actions. For instance, a friend has been promoted. To show empathy, someone would probably express excitement about the news, offer to celebrate, and feel genuinely happy for them. Even though the event that's occurring is not directly impacting you, you can still experience joy for them and with them.

Being an empath, however, takes things a step further than that. Empaths absorb other people's emotions into themselves. They can feel those emotions so deeply and profoundly that it affects them on a psychological level and maybe even physically. Some empaths are so in tune with their surrounding environments that they no longer require external cues. What does that mean?

They can pick up on the energies around them without the other person uttering a single word. This may sound like a superpower, but this gift comes with a few drawbacks. One of them is feeling the loss of control over one's own emotions and being susceptible to uncontrolled mood alterations depending on the energies of the people surrounding you. Some people may even find it challenging to ascertain whether their feelings are theirs or someone else's.

To fully understand the term, you need to examine both the scientific and the spiritual aspects.

Empathy According to Science and Neurology

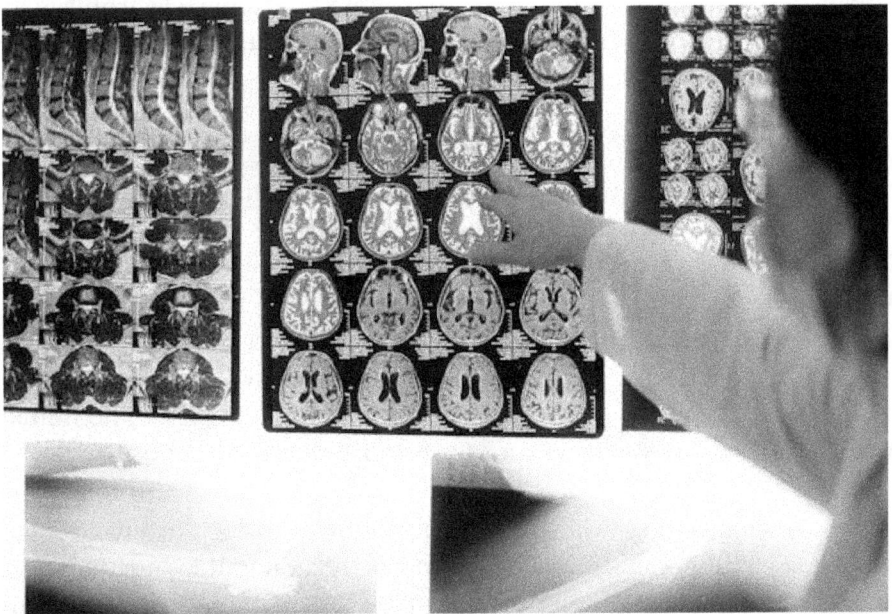

Neurology gives us insight into how the brain works with empathy.[2]

A number of notable scientists have explored the intricacies behind the practice of showing empathy. Among those are Christian Keysers, Valeria Gazzola, and Judith Orloff, MD, a psychiatrist and a self-identified empath. The topic was researched extensively from a scientific point of view, and its interpretation was narrowed down to 5 main explanations:

The Mirror Neuron: It's been proven that within the brain, there is a cluster of cells primarily responsible for compassion. Acting as reflective surfaces, these cells enable you to mirror the emotions of people around you.

These neurons jump to action when an outside trigger occurs. For example, if someone is witnessing another's pain or desolation, these neurons would mimic the emotion in their brain, making them feel the same sensation. If you see someone in a celebratory mood, it's expected to find yourself catching on to their joy and joining in. Empaths tend to have a hyperactive or slightly overly sensitive version of these neurons, enabling them to connect to the other person's feelings more intensely.

In other cases, people with underactive mirror neurons find it hard to relate to others' emotions. These people usually have what is called an "empathy deficit disorder."

Electromagnetic Fields: This explanation relies on the fact that the human body, specifically the heart and brain, can emit electromagnetic fields. At the HeartMath Institute, they believe that information can travel while carrying the thoughts and emotions of others. Naturally, empaths could easily feel flooded by the onslaught of information transmitted due to their sensitivity.

These electromagnetic fields are not just transmitted from one person to another. Empaths are often sensitive to changes in the sun and the earth's fields, too. These changes can easily impact the state of mind and energy.

Emotional Contagion or Resonance: This theory rings true with the expression "contagious laughter." This concept pretty much sums up this explanation. There is a reason a lot of life coaches emphasize the human need to surround oneself with positivity and people with a positive line of thinking.

In a normal setting, when a person starts expressing anxiety or anger within a circle of people, others will start catching on to the same emotions and mimicking them. For empaths, in these situations where they are forced to deal with others' negative outbursts, they need to arm themselves with the tools to stay grounded and centered.

Increased Dopamine Sensitivity: Dopamine is a hormone responsible for activating the pleasure response. An interesting finding showed a distinction between introverted and extroverted empaths. It is believed that introverted empaths are much more sensitive to the dopamine neurotransmitter than extroverted ones.

At first glance, this may seem like a bad thing. However, it's quite the opposite. It basically means that introverts can feel contentment easier than extroverts, which tracks with the common stereotype of how introverts enjoy their private time and quiet activities. As for extroverts, they're on the other side of the spectrum, in constant need of external triggers for dopamine rushes to satisfy their need for bliss.

Synesthesia: This is also known as the " mirror-touch synesthesia." Many of history's greats are associated with this concept, such as Sir Isaac Newton and Itzhak Perlman. It is a neurological state of the brain where two senses collide together. For example, someone can listen to soft music and immediately envision the colors blue or green, like a calm sea, or wide pastures, or maybe a combination of words and taste. You hear the name of a person you dislike or a word you're not fond of and immediately taste a metallic sensation in your mouth, kind of like when people say, "I was so furious I saw red."

People who are able to experience this phenomenon can actually feel the emotions of others in physical form within their own bodies.

Types of Empathy

Empathy can be categorized into 3 main types: Cognitive, emotional, and compassionate.

1. **Cognitive Empathy:** It is the ability to put oneself in someone else's shoes. For example, a friend informs an empath that they've lost a close family member and then starts crying. With cognitive empathy, the empath's response will be a caring one, like saying, "I'm sorry for your loss, I get how you feel, and I understand it must be very hard for you."
2. **Emotional Empathy:** This response takes it one level higher. If faced with a negative situation, a person can easily have an emotional reaction and get distressed. They may feel a deep need to offer help to the person they're interacting with. If the situation is a happy one, that also applies
3. **Compassionate Empathy:** While most modern research exclusively categorizes empathy into the previous two types, some argue that there is a third main type. This concept encapsulates the perfect balance between cognitive and emotional empathy.

People who are able to practice compassionate empathy don't just connect to others on an intellectual and emotional level but also maintain a level-headedness that allows them to take action that benefits the other party. They are able to regulate their own emotions and help with the regulation of others without being swept away by outside energies. They can apply logic and see the world through the other person's eyes while creating a safe space for them to express themselves.

For example, if they're approached by a person from work who is distraught from unfair treatment by their manager, they will acknowledge their emotions by saying, for instance, "I know how important this job is for you; you must be infuriated by the way you're being treated, I support you 100%." Once the friend has calmed down enough, they would then proceed with, " Walk me through the issue, and we'll figure out a plan of action together."

In essence, this type of empathy is the best of both worlds.

Additional Types of Empathy (Affective and Somatic)

Compared to the three previous types, affective and somatic empathy are less commonly acknowledged.

Affective Empathy is the ability to acknowledge and share the experiences and emotions of others without being emotionally engaged.

Somatic Empathy, on the other hand, is the polar opposite. Not only does the empath engage emotionally with the other person, but they may also experience a physical reaction, like having a knot in their stomach, if another person is nervous or anxious.

People with somatic empathy can experience physical reactions such as pain in their stomachs.[8]

The Spiritual Aspect of Empathy

Some people refer to empaths as "mind readers" due to their high sensitivity and sharp natural instinct to detect the changing waves of energy in others. They are usually in high demand in jobs that require a high level of intuition, like therapists, teachers, and, at times, healers. However, they also are most likely to experience burnout from the immense amount of emotions that they absorb on a daily basis, leaving them depleted unless they safeguard themselves with healthy practices that block other people's energies from hijacking their psyche and physical body.

Why Do Empaths Absorb the Emotions and Energy of Others?

Empaths usually see and experience the world with a "we" mentality. That is referred to as the collective consciousness. Empaths naturally long to be in a community that allows for unconscious merging between the people existing in their inner circles and themselves.

Consequently, that also causes them to pick up on the unpleasant parts of others' energies, such as grief, anger, and sadness.

The most basic human form is composed of energy. The 3 main systems are auras, chakras, and meridians.

1. **Auras:** An Aura is a sphere of energy consisting of several layers surrounding the body, connecting it and interacting with the Earth's atmosphere. If the aura is healthy, it can protect you from absorbing harmful energies and maintain the proper functionality of all your other systems.

The Aura is the energy surrounding you.[4]

2. **Chakras:** The human body has hundreds of chakras in and around it. However, most healers focus on the main seven. These are in charge of maintaining and regulating different sets of physical organs and emotions within the body. Each chakra has a different level of activity. When one is blocked or out of balance, it can cause a person to feel a wide range of uncomfortable sensations, from mild exhaustion to major health problems.

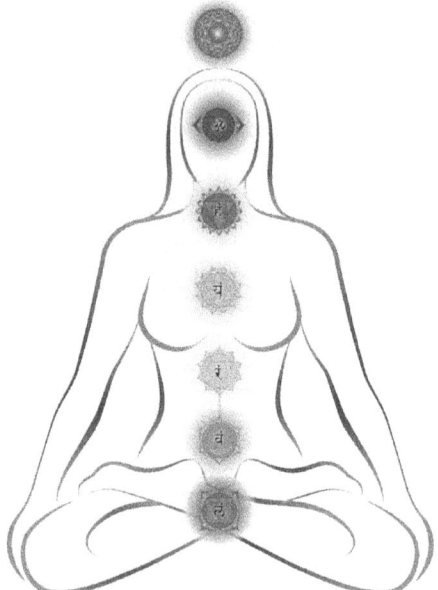

The Chakras are different energy centers in the body.⁵

3. **Meridians:** In different cultures, they are known as Chi, Prana, or Qi. Meridians are in charge of carrying energy and affect every major system in the body, like the immune, lymphatic, skeletal, muscular, and so on. If a Chi is blocked or out of balance, the system it's responsible for its health becomes vulnerable to disease.

Vibrational Sensitivity

Each human being has a specific vibration, and every sensation has its own vibration.

Vibrations measure the energy system as a whole using hertz, which is the same unit of measure for sound and frequency. The different levels usually determine the state of your energy system's health. People with high frequencies usually experience contentment and thrive, while lower levels can easily cause a person to fall ill and be vulnerable to receiving negative energies.

Past Lives and Soul Missions

Some cultures honor the belief that the soul transcends time and space and that each person on this earth has lived a thousand lives and met most of the people they know today in one of their past lives. These cultures also believe that certain people, most likely empaths, can connect with these past lives and fulfill their sacred soul missions through exercises like meditation.

A similar concept is sometimes referred to as an Indigo Adult. Someone with a unique set of skills and features that would arrive to bring forth the evolution of the species. It is thought that empaths have a stronger connection to their past lives and soul missions than others due to their high level of sensitivity.

This sensitivity is the main reason they have a natural talent for energy healing and light work. This natural gift usually means that empaths unconsciously heal their surrounding environments and the people around them.

For untrained empaths, this may cause a problem. That's because as they absorb the outside energies into themselves to allow their surroundings to have more suitable and higher levels of vibration, they may accidentally block their own systems. This can cause a number of issues, which can be anything from hormonal instabilities to general exhaustion and sickness.

An empath can sometimes be easily spotted in a crowded room, as people are inclined to gravitate towards them and be near their energies, openly sharing their experiences and stories with them.

This, in part, is one of the reasons why empaths are known as light workers or bringers of light. They are basically individuals who have decided to make the world a better place by consciously existing *within it*. Their power to sense feelings in others and intuitive and psychic sense of just knowing things and interpreting their surrounding energy sets them apart from the crowd.

The Science Behind Empathic Sensitivity

Empaths can experience, from time to time, the side effects of taking on other people's emotional baggage. People who often experience this may have what is called a Sensory Processing Sensitivity (SPS). People with SPS are usually also referred to as HSPs (Highly Sensitive People).

The mirror neurons concept tends to manifest heavily when those two scenarios exist. From a biological perspective, empaths have a much more active mirror neuron system than an ordinary person, which explains the extra sensitivity to their surroundings. This enhanced activity allows empaths to accurately read facial gestures and body language like their own personal map.

HSPs tend to have a higher capacity to absorb the emotions and energies of others, as well as a greater capacity for empathy. They can sense conflict and tension as soon as they enter the room, and their brains immediately begin reacting to it. This isn't always a positive thing, especially with negative emotions.

People with SPS can process the information given to them on a deeper level than ordinary empaths. They can easily be over-stimulated and pick up on the most subtle changes in the atmosphere surrounding them.

Autonomic Nervous System (ANS)

A person's capacity to show empathy is closely related to the autonomic nervous system (ANS). This system is primarily responsible for how people react to stress and whether or not they can manage it and relax themselves back to a sense of safety. Consequently, this also relates to whether the Vagus nerve is healthy or not.

The Vagus Nerve is basically the tool in the body that gives you the information you need to determine if you are in danger or not. It comprises two circuits: the Ventral Vagal Circuit and the Dorsal Vagal Circuit.

The Ventral Vagal Circuit is also called the social engagement system. It is responsible for the feeling of safety and for the ability to effectively communicate and listen to others. It's mainly connected to the muscles residing above the midriff, controlling and guiding facial expressions and verbal interactions.

The Dorsal Vagal Circuit is situated below the midriff, mainly controlling the organs responsible for digestion. If a person feels unthreatened, the two circuits harmonize together to create a sense of relaxation. On the opposite end, if a person is alert to an impending danger, the Dorsal Vagal Circuit can create a sense of nausea and dizziness.

Since empathy means being able to pick up on others' emotions, by doing so, the nervous system momentarily assumes that energy belongs to the empath, not coming from an outer source. In situations when these emotions are unpleasant, the nervous system translates them into threats. That throws it – and the body's physical state – out of balance because the vagus nerve becomes disrupted, and the body automatically assumes a defensive state.

It takes time and conscious practice to be able to regulate a disoriented vagus nerve.

The Gut-Brain Connection

Also known as the gut-brain axis, this connection is responsible for the chemical signals sent between the central nervous system and the gastrointestinal tract. The axis ensures there is continuous communication moving back and forth through the immune system, hormones, and neurotransmitters. Figuring out the mechanics of the connection allows you to better manage your mental health through making healthy dietary options.

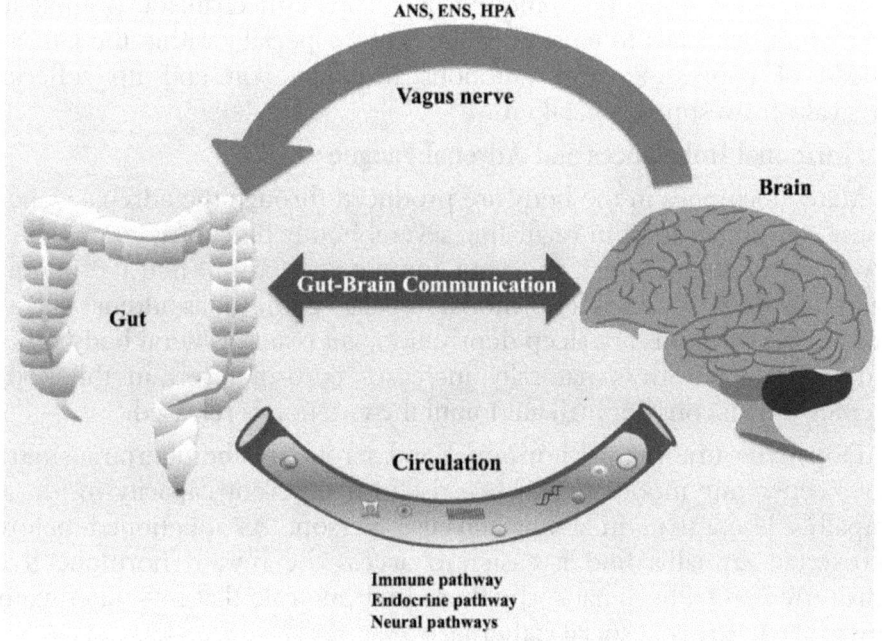

The Gut-Brain Connection.*

What goes through the mouth directly impacts the state of your brain. If a person chooses a high-fiber diet, the microbes in the gut will be nourished. A happy microbiome can sway the mood more towards the positive side, which leaves a similar impact on mental capacity and mood.

If the gut-brain axis breaks down for any reason, whether neurological, like stress and anxiety, or physical, like a poor diet, that can result in major health issues and a lot of emotional distress.

With empaths, this risk is even higher due to their intense sensitivity to the circumjacent energy.

Overworked Nervous System: At times that require heavy social interactions, the body flicks continuously between fight or flight modes. This limits the blood flow from reaching your digestive system efficiently. As time passes, it can develop into chronic digestive ailments that are resistant to normal remedies.

Physical Responses Triggered By Emotions: Many empaths reported that they can feel others' pain in their own bodies. That is not an exaggeration. An empath's nervous system internalizes the energy they receive from others and directs it towards the digestive system, which triggers physical responses.

Suppressing Emotions: A common mistake empaths make is pushing down and smothering their emotions as a coping mechanism. Bottling up these emotions leads to tension in the body, especially within the gut. So, instead of expressing your emotions healthily, you end up suffering physically from suppressing them.

Hormonal Imbalances and Adrenal Fatigue

Many hormones in the body are produced through the adrenal glands. These hormones assist in regulating several bodily functions; among those is your response to stress and your immune system. When the adrenal gland falls short, it causes a hormonal imbalance known as adrenal fatigue. Among its symptoms are sleep deprivation, gut issues, general body aches, and exhaustion. Stress naturally increases cortisol levels in the body, keeping it on a constant high alert until the emotion is released.

Dopamine (the reward hormone) and serotonin (the neurotransmitter that keeps your mood in check) exist in a different capacity inside an empath's brain than in a non-sensitive person. As mentioned before, introverted empaths find it easier to access the reward hormone than extroverted empaths. That's why there isn't one rule that says all empaths thrive or retrogress in social gatherings.

More often than not, within an empath's brain, they have a more effective variant of the serotonin transporter (the 5-HTTLPR), which clears the serotonin from the brain faster than others. This quick action usually leaves them more vulnerable to frequent mood swings and lessens their emotional stability.

The Blessings and Challenges of Being an Empath

Like all things in the world, there are two sides to every coin.

Blessings

- **Creativity:** The deeper a person can connect to things, the easier inspiration comes to them. Empaths are talented artists, musicians, and writers. They are able to express thoughts and sensations with unique complexity and extravagance.
- **Healing Powers:** With heightened senses, empaths can easily sense others' discomfort and frustrations. Finding the right remedy for people would come naturally to an empath, whether that remedy is physical, psychological, or spiritual. Empaths excel at being natural healers, caregivers, and counselors.
- **Sharp Intuition:** Empaths can assess situations and know things about people through their "gut feeling." When followed effectively, they can dodge problems, work with different mentalities, and make positive, strong decisions.
- **Special Connection to Nature:** One of the perks of being an empath is that being around animals and in nature allows them to center themselves and keep their energies balanced. Because of their inviting energy, animals are drawn towards them just as often as people are.

Challenges

- **Setting Boundaries:** Empaths often have trouble with setting and maintaining boundaries. The word "no" is very difficult to come by for them. This usually results in emotional depletion, burnout, and putting their own self-care on standby. This can also make empaths more prone to manipulations.
- **Emotional Overwhelm:** If an empath doesn't employ tactics to help block outside energies and emotions, or at least navigate them effectively without holding on to them in their bodies, they can experience serious reactions. Feeling anxious, overloaded, and exhausted on an emotional and physical level are among the downsides.

- **A Need for Solitude:** Empaths gravitate towards alone time more than others. This may translate to others as them being aloof. However, all it means is that their emotional batteries have been depleted from taking on everyone else's emotions, and they just need to recharge.
- **Energy Vampires:** Because of their inviting energy, empaths might find themselves surrounded by individuals with a lot of negative energy. These people take advantage of empaths' willingness to be of service and listen constantly, feeding off their healing qualities and energy and transmitting their less-than-desirable energy back to them. That can leave an empath in a constant state of emotional exhaustion if they don't put up protective walls to safeguard themselves, figuratively and literally.

Quiz: Am I an Empath?

Answer the below questions with "Yes" or "No."

1. Have you ever been described as an over-sensitive person, timid, or introverted?
2. Do you easily get overwhelmed or feel uneasy?
3. Do I often feel out of place or struggling to fit in?
4. Do you feel your energy drained in crowded places and feel the need to recharge alone?
5. Are you easily startled?
6. Do you feel overstimulated by sounds, scents, or continuous chatter?
7. Do you require a long time to recover after dealing with narcissists, difficult people, or energy vampires?
8. Are you sensitive to any chemicals or can't stand certain textures of fabrics?
9. Do you feel your temperature rising when dealing with stressful situations?
10. Are you afraid of intimacy and being boxed in a relationship?
11. Do you have strong reactions to caffeinated drinks or medicine?
12. Do you feel pain easily?
13. Do conflicts or loud noises make you ill?
14. Do you prefer being alone over being with a group of people or acquaintances?
15. Do you absorb other people's stress, emotions, or symptoms?
16. Do you feel recharged after spending time in nature?
17. Do you prefer spending time in the country or small cities rather than larger, crowded cities?
18. Do you feel stressed out when handling more than one task at the same time and prefer to finish each in turn?
19. Do you enjoy individual one-to-one interactions or smaller groups over bigger gatherings?
20. Do you prefer having your own ride so you can leave whenever you like?

How to Calculate the Results:

- If you answered "yes" to five questions or less, you're at least partially an empath.
- If you answered "yes" to six to ten questions, you have some empathic tendencies.
- If you answered "yes" to eleven to fifteen, you have stronger than average empathic tendencies.
- Answering "yes" to more than fifteen questions means you are a true empath.

Chapter 2: Empaths vs Highly Sensitive Persons (HSPs)

Empaths are often dismissed or mislabeled as being highly sensitive individuals, as they're incredibly susceptive to stimuli. While this trait makes them stand out and misunderstood, using the term *highly sensitive people* with empaths is not accurate. While all empaths are highly sensitive, not all highly sensitive people (highly sensitive persons or HSPs) are empaths.

You need to know the difference between an empath and an HSP.'

This chapter aims to clear up the differences between these two groups, highlighting their characteristics, differences, and slight overlaps. By reading it, you'll gain a deeper understanding of empath and HSP traits, which is crucial for raising awareness of your own characteristics, learning to manage energy, setting boundaries, and much more. At the end of the chapter, you can assess whether you belong to one group or the other or, perhaps, both.

The Empath Spectrum

One of the main reasons for the misidentification of empaths is that empathy exists on a spectrum, from those who aren't receptive to other people's emotions and experiences to those who can pick up on others' feelings without even intending to. Basic emotional awareness varies greatly among individuals. Narcissists, for example, do not have any clues about how others may feel or have any regard for others' feelings. This puts them at the opposite end of the spectrum from highly perceptive true empaths. In the middle of the spectrum are indifferent individuals. Going slightly toward the full-blown empaths are the people with basic emotional awareness. Lying between them and the true empaths are the highly sensitive individuals.

Besides narcissists and other individuals suffering from empathy-deficiency disorders, most people feel general empathy, which isn't the same as being an empath. Empathizing with someone is a naturally learned trait, which only means keeping their feelings, thoughts, needs, and issues in mind. Unlike true empaths and highly sensitive individuals, most people who feel general empathy do not pick up on other people's feelings or perceptions of experiences.

What Is a Highly Sensitive Person (HSP)?

After extensive research on high sensitivity in people in the 1990s, American psychologist Dr. Elaine Aron coined the term Highly Sensitive Person (HSP). The birth of this term was a result of an in-depth evaluation of personality traits, including that of sensory-processing sensitivity, which HSPs were found to have. This affirmed that highly sensitive individuals have intense emotional reactivity and sensitivity to every external and internal stimulus. While other people who may pick up on these stimuli don't spend much time processing them before dismissing them as a normal part of their environment, HSPs find the stimuli overwhelming. For the same reason, their stimulus-reaction interactions and their life in general become complex.

Today, psychologists estimate that 15-20% of the world population is affected by sensory-processing sensitivity, making them fall into the class of HSPs.

However, knowing these individuals are often misunderstood, and hence, many won't seek guidance on navigating their challenges, some therapists claim that the true number of HSPs in the world could be even higher.

Yet, despite all the challenges, being an HSP can have its advantages, so finding out whether you have this trait is a journey worth pursuing. Moreover, by focusing on the positive, HSPs can learn to navigate life more successfully than individuals who don't have the sensory sensitivity trait. After all, it's an attribute that allows people to stop and analyze their perceptions, which reduces the chances of mistakes. They may also reflect on their lives, going through memories of events like one would watch a movie.

Besides not being quick to act, highly sensitive individuals have plenty of other characteristics, too. As they process information deeply, HSPs often overthink situations and experiences. They become lost in the tiny details and can't move forward by simply dealing with the situation at hand.

HSPs are reactive to physical stimuli. They react strongly to sensory stimuli like movement, light, or music. This often means they have profound emotional responses to music, art, and beauty. On the flip side, it also signifies that they can get easily overwhelmed by bright lights, intense smells, loud noises, and even uncomfortable clothes.

HSPs react strongly to music.*

HSPs are also wired to interact more with all the information around them, including social situations and emotional landscapes. This could help them develop deeper interpersonal connections, although they may find it harder to establish relationships due to their differences with people without sensory sensitivity.

Having intense emotional reactions to their environment can also mean that an HSP isn't often able to watch emotionally charged movies or TV shows or be near people who thrive on creating conflicts and situations where intense feelings arise.

For example, an HSP likely won't do well working alongside a colleague who criticizes or makes offensive remarks about everyone, evoking intense negative emotions in others all the time. Their other coworkers may be able to brush off the harsh words and focus on doing their job, but an HSP will likely feel drained and unmotivated to keep working.

Just like HSPs may feel exhausted after being exposed to a dynamic environment full of physical stimuli, they may feel they don't have the mental energy to navigate socially elaborate situations where a lot of interactions are happening at once. If they're forced to endure these situations, they'll require more time to recharge. Speaking of recharging, HSPs often need plenty of downtime, preferably somewhere they can retreat to in solitude and not be around others.

HSPs are introverts by nature. They prefer to have as few interactions with others as possible. Instead of being exposed to environments where they don't feel at ease and have to deal with other people all the time, they thrive in positions where they can focus on discovering beauty and information they find comforting or enjoyable.

HSPs don't handle changes well, either. Most changes come with a host of unknown stimuli to process and handle, which doesn't come easily. This applies to environmental and social shifts, both of which HSPs prefer to avoid. Likewise, they'll do whatever they can to avoid situations where they feel overwhelmed, especially if they've gained awareness of their increased sensitivity and reactivity to specific stimuli. These people often compensate (or try to) by finding beauty in everything and everyone and disregarding all the ugliness they can pick up on. When joined with their appreciation of art, the characteristics of wanting to bring out or create something beautiful can drive HSPs to explore their creativity and artistic skills.

Even though an HSP's brain may be working to process many stimuli simultaneously, it doesn't allow multitasking. If a person tries performing several tasks requiring complete focus, they're likely to get overwhelmed. As they feel a higher level of empathy for others, they may try multitasking to help others, but in the end, they will need help finishing the tasks they jumped to help out with in the first place.

Another characteristic that drives HSPs toward having richer inner lives is the ability to be by themselves for longer periods. They don't feel the need to remain connected with others. They don't need other people to toss thoughts around. They can do that themselves. They can have long conversations with their inner self and reach a more profound conclusion than they would by conversing with someone who doesn't seek to understand them.

There is nothing worse for HSPs than knowing they spend so much time analyzing everything about others, situations, and environments, only for others not to take the time to consider their feelings, thoughts, and views. Unfortunately, this often makes HSPs feel like they are outsiders in a society where everyone else functions the same way.

As they are built a little differently, they may feel there is something wrong with them. Some feel ashamed or guilty over being different and reacting far more intensely than others. Worse, some HSPs are made to feel this way, most often by indifferent individuals or those who seek to take advantage of them. This can lead to isolation and loneliness, but it doesn't have to be this way. Just because you don't know anyone like you, it doesn't mean you're alone. After all, 15-20% isn't a negligible portion of the population.

Moreover, while HSPs react more intensely to stimuli, they likely won't absorb others' emotions as empaths do.

In other words, HSPs may find it easier to navigate certain situations than empaths. They may also avoid being taken advantage of, while empaths will more likely fall victim to emotional manipulation tactics often employed by those on the other end of the empath spectrum (for example, narcissists are notorious manipulators). Since HSPs stay empathetic without taking on others' emotions, they aren't as easy to manipulate. Still, they risk being affected by empathy fatigue, which stems from being compassionate toward those whose feelings are put before their own.

Ethan's story

"Growing up, I was always told I was a bit sensitive.

Some would add that this isn't a bad thing, while others made it clear that a little boy shouldn't be so sensitive about everything.

While I knew I wasn't like other little boys, I didn't understand why or what this meant. I only understood that I had to become (or at least appear to be) tougher. As a result, I grew up to be a person who, albeit still sensitive, kept their sensitivity hidden behind a seemingly stoic approach to life.

As I got older, I noticed that, besides being easily startled and needing time away from busy interactions, I also became able to pick up on other people's feelings. Their emotions didn't really affect me. I just found it strange how easily I noticed that someone next to me was tense or anxious. Still, I just assumed I was more observant than others. After others noticed this, too, I became the go-to person those around me would talk to when feeling stressed. This was even more overwhelming. I didn't mind listening to them. It was just that being constantly around people made me feel drained.

I was in my mid-20s when I discovered that I wasn't the only person with these experiences. That was the first time I read about highly sensitive people. It was astonishing how much everything I learned about HSP characteristics resonated with me and my earlier experiences. At the same time, it was comforting to know that others are in the same shoes and have to navigate the same challenges I do. It gave me hope that I can talk to others without being misunderstood or told to toughen up."

Key Trait Differences Between Empaths and HSPs

	Empaths	HSPs
Information Processing	Absorb and process emotional information from others on a deeper level	Absorb and process what's being said on a deeper level, but not so much others' emotions
Stimulation Source	Most sensitive to emotional stimuli from others	Extremely sensitive to all sensory stimuli, including emotions
Extrovert/Introvert	Can be introverts or extroverts	Strictly introverts
Boundary Setting	Difficulty separating emotions from others'	Can become overwhelmed by others' emotions by knowing that they're not their own
Other Abilities	Heightened intuition	Intuition may be even stronger
Sensitivity to positive experiences	Not overly sensitive to positive experiences	Highly sensitive to both negative and positive experiences

Who Are Empaths?

Unlike highly sensitive people, empaths can experience other people's feelings on a deeper level. Due to their heightened sensitivity, they pick up on the feelings, just like HSPs, but their interactions with these emotions don't stop there. Empaths absorb everything, including symptoms of emotional, mental, and physical traumas. What makes empaths so different that they can do this? There are a few factors that can explain their ability to internalize others' feelings and experiences.

Firstly, they often rely on their intuition. Awareness and reflection are both traits closely associated with intuition.

Empaths tend to have strong intuition.⁹

Relying on your intuition means you are attuned to the world around you as well as your inner self. You're aware of what's happening and become automatically attuned to other people's moods. So, when empaths pick up on other people's emotions, they internalize them intuitively. To them, this comes naturally, even when it's harmful to them.

Many times, empaths absorb other people's negative moods, which fosters negative feelings in them. Moreover, empaths, like HSPs, feel everything to the extreme. Why? They can't rationalize that the negativity they picked up on from others doesn't have anything to do with them. If they absorb anxiety or anger, empaths will be anxious and angry, too, even if they have no reason to be. This often leads them to be exhausted and drained of positive energy.

Over time, they start to feel the impact of all the negativity they absorb and experience fatigue, stress, depression, and other symptoms of declining mental and emotional health. Empaths may even experience physical symptoms from absorbing energy (e.g., headaches, fatigue).

If the negativity isn't countered with positivity, empaths can also be driven to addictive behaviors. This may happen if an empath doesn't learn to trust their gut or set proper boundaries for keeping emotional and energetic influences at bay. Learning to trust their intuition can help empaths build better relationships and avoid falling victim to narcissists and other negative people. Like HSPs, empaths are often targeted by manipulative individuals whose interactions drain their energy. Besides making empaths feel physically, mentally, and emotionally exhausted, narcissists and others who lack empathy can make them feel unworthy of love, attention, and validation.

Empaths who learn to counter negative energies and reground themselves after interacting with others' negative feelings, moods, and energies won't be affected by these as much and will be able to thrive. Others may surround themselves with peace and love so as to avoid coming across energies they can internalize without intending to.

However, not all empaths will choose to engage with just positivity, and the reason behind this is pretty simple. They are givers. They love to listen to others and embrace other perspectives. They listen wholeheartedly, ready to jump in and offer whatever others need. They also love to nurture and comfort others, so if someone around them is going through tough times, the empath will be there to offer a shoulder to lean on.

Empaths love to listen wholeheartedly.[10]

Unfortunately, empaths can become overwhelmed in relationships due to their innate need to give all they have and their ability to feel so much. After being enmeshed with the other party's feelings in the relationship, some may feel like they don't even know where they begin and where the other person ends. They feel like they have lost their identity, which is a frightening experience. They may even back out of the relationship because they feel so overwhelmed. After this experience, they may avoid relationships altogether because they can't risk becoming so deeply connected to another person again.

Other empaths may avoid relationships because they got their feelings hurt in a previous relationship or have watched someone close to them have their feelings hurt. Both are likely to happen to empaths. After all, these individuals are constantly told they are overly sensitive or shouldn't care so much about other people's feelings.

Telling empaths to toughen up or that having a big heart is a negative trait reinforces the impact of the negativity they absorb. Their feelings get hurt when they give so much, and it's not appreciated. For example, if they offer assistance to a distraught friend and the friend rejects them, saying they don't need help and shouldn't even be offered any, the empath can get offended. They feel like they've done nothing wrong because extending assistance comes naturally to them. They do it from the kindness of their (very big) heart and don't see why their friend wouldn't accept it.

Besides being able to listen to their gut feelings, empaths have highly tuned senses that pick up physical stimuli like smells, sounds, textures, and sights. Just like HSPs, empaths can become overwhelmed by all these stimuli. They may feel drained by crowds and emotionally intense environments.

Empaths can be both extroverted and introverted. Those belonging to the latter category often find it emotionally draining to be around others because the more people are around them, the harder their empathic ability works. They like to hang around with one person at a time or a small group. Extroverted empaths don't get so easily overwhelmed but may still prefer not to be around too many people most of the time. The less time they spend in busy places, the fewer the chances to pick up on someone's emotions and the more uninterrupted experiences they can enjoy. After interactions, both introvert and extrovert empaths need alone time to recharge. For extroverts, this may only be a few minutes they spend without feeling the need to respond to others. Introverted empaths often plan their time off and take a little longer before being there for others again. They prefer to know they can come and go as they please.

Sabia's story

"When I was a child, I both loved and hated school. I loved it because I always enjoyed learning new things, and hated it because I had very few positive interactions with teachers and other children.

I felt constantly criticized and undermined. I was always told that I take everything personally. It made me feel like I couldn't be successful at school and later on in the career I wanted to build for myself. I felt that everyone expected me to be someone different, and I spent years trying to figure out how to achieve this. I did this until I learned there was no reason to be someone different because there was nothing wrong with who I was. I was built a little differently and given a little higher dose of empathy than most people.

I also learned that being an empath meant I could absorb other people's feelings. This made me realize why I felt so overwhelmed ever since I first started struggling in school. Imagine trying to deal with your own issues and picking up on everything everyone else around you was dealing with, too! It's no wonder I took everything personally. I couldn't help it. Everything felt personal to me, even when it wasn't.

Over time, I accepted that I can understand people on a much deeper level. Most people who experience general empathy can envision what others may feel in certain situations. They can sort of put themselves in others' shoes. I don't have to imagine. I simply know because I feel it, too. At one point, when I was learning how to navigate life as an empath, I struggled to separate my own feelings from others. Now, I have reached the point where I know that when I feel like something bad is happening to me, I automatically check myself to see whether it's happening to me or I'm picking up on someone else's bad experiences. Now that I know not to constantly expose myself, I have begun to embrace my empathy as a power to behold and not something to be ashamed of."

Can You Be Both?

The short answer is yes.

You can be both a highly sensitive person and an empath. Many empaths experience heightened sensory sensitivity. This is often the first sign they pick on about being different from others.

Yet, not all HSPs are empaths. Some simply remain sensitive and experience a somewhat higher emotional awareness. The reason for these differences lies in the depth of the empath's experiences. They don't just pick up on emotions. They pick up on energy. Energy fills every space and permeates every living and nonliving entity in the universe. Empaths experience this universal energy, including all the changes and shifts in it, at a profound level. They intuitively connect to others' energies, can influence energy fields, and become influenced by them themselves. Seasoned empaths can sense and differentiate between the energies of living beings, spirits, and other entities from realms beyond the earthly one.

Self-Assessment Quiz

Are you wondering whether you are an HSP, an empath, or both? Check out the quiz below to learn where you fit in on the empath spectrum.

1. Do you often find yourself making arrangements (or excuses) to avoid situations in which you usually get overwhelmed?
2. Are the first things you notice when walking into a space unusual smells, sounds, or sights?
3. Do you often stop to appreciate beautiful pieces of art?
4. Would you describe your inner life as complex?

5. As a child, have you been told by teachers, classmates, or parents that you're too sensitive?
6. Do you find it difficult to balance doing several tasks at once?
7. Do you prefer to avoid watching violent programs on TV?
8. Do you feel other people's emotions like they're your own?
9. Do you feel drained after interacting with others?
10. Do you rely on your gut to tell you how you or someone else is feeling?
11. When you notice that someone is going through a tough time, do you have the desire to help them overcome their challenges?
12. Do you find setting boundaries difficult in your interpersonal relationships?
13. Are you an outgoing person who occasionally needs time for themselves?
14. Do you have emotions that feel like they're not your own, or you aren't sure whether they're yours or someone else's?
15. Do you often feel overstimulated by busy, chaotic situations and environments?
16. Do you feel misunderstood by others or like you're always standing out because you're different from everyone else around you?
17. Do others describe you as a compassionate and caring person?
18. Do you need time to recharge after being social?

If you answered questions 1-7 with a yes, you're likely an HSP.

If you answered the questions 8-14 with a yes, you're most likely an empath.

However, if you responded to questions 15-18 with a yes, you may be both an empath and an HSP.

Chapter 3: ENERGY WORK I: Energy Anatomy (Chakras, the Aura, and Your Unique Frequency)

Understanding your personal energy system supports your mental and physical health. In this chapter, you will discover the foundational elements of your personal energy system: the chakras, auras, and your unique frequency. You will learn practical exercises to strengthen and balance your energy anatomy and flow.

When you understand the anatomy of energy, you're in a better position to care for yourself.[11]

Understanding Energy Anatomy

Everything is energy, from the air you inhale to your words and actions. In India, energy is called Prana. In China, it is known as Chi, and in Japan, it is referred to as Qi. All these words describe the energy field fundamental in creating and preserving life. This pure life force makes an entity feel alive. Think of a corpse and how it was once alive with a soul and spirit. That is energy.

Every living thing has an energy field, which stores and replaces energy based on thoughts, feelings, and emotional needs. How successful you are at maintaining a positive mental state determines the health of your energy anatomy. Just as a diet lacking in nutrients can affect your physical anatomy, a disrupted energy field can cause problems for your energy anatomy, leading to depression and even physical ailments. It shows just how much energy can transform your health.

Most empaths struggle with managing their energy field due to having such a high absorption rate. An empath's ability to feel deeply is directly tied to their energy field.

Your connection to your consciousness may be slightly heightened compared to others because your frequency is determined by your energy field. Empaths are highly attuned to the energy around them, making them aware of others' feelings, and may attract more than they'd like into their energy field.

By nature, your energy is soothing to others, which is a wonderful gift. The downside is that other people's thoughts and emotions enter your energy field like an electric current consuming your presence. Absorbing others' energy like a sponge without boundaries can drain you, leading to a low vibrational state.

The Four Main Subtle Bodies

Energy flows through the four main subtle bodies, working together in intricate patterns to create vibrational resonance. They are an ever-changing painting on the canvas that is your anatomy. Depending on how well you nurture the art of living, the colors with which you paint your life can be dull or vibrant.

1. The Physical Body

The physical body is the material form of your energy anatomy and the most obvious example of your energy's existence. Your life experiences – from joys to sorrows and how far you've traveled in the external world – appear on the physical body as scars, wrinkles, and smile lines. Your body feels, expresses, and channels energy through this primary medium. To maintain the physical body's endurance, be aware of energy symptoms, such as fatigue and body aches. Combat these with good nutrition and yoga to maintain a healthy balance of rest and movement.

2. The Emotional Body

This layer of your subtle body holds all your feelings and past traumas. It pulsates when you experience love, excitement, fear, sadness, etc. Learning what your feelings are trying to tell you is your compass guiding you towards an emotional body that experiences healthy interactions. Then, you can ascertain that the feelings residing within aren't holding your emotional health back. Instead, they advise you on what emotional setbacks you've had and need work, propelling you toward a stronger emotional well-being that can weather any storm.

Your emotional body needs guidance if you experience signs of getting overwhelmed and mood swings, which typically result from retaining others' emotions. Consider journaling and emotional release techniques and practice self-love through affirmations and gratitude.

3. The Mental Body

The mental body governs the thoughts that determine your reality. It can build or break your mental health. While thoughts can put out the fire in your body, they can also be used to ignite your passion. By mastering your thoughts, you can create the blueprint for your energy instead of having your thoughts control your energy flow.

Your mental subtle body provides many insights, from what causes energy blockage to building resilience. Negative thoughts, overthinking, self-doubt, and anxiety can clutter your mind. However, taking control of your thoughts through meditation, breathwork, and reprogramming limiting beliefs will attract good energy and determine your new reality. Being intentional in your thoughts is transformative for the mental body. It balances your energy, allowing creativity, resilience, and logic to flourish.

4. The Spiritual Body

The spiritual body transcends the physical, emotional, and mental bodies and connects you to an ethereal realm full of intuition and potential. It encapsulates your purpose beyond other subtle bodies. Even though it's harder to track, this layer holds immense power. It is the core of your being and ascends you to higher dimensions of consciousness. Nurturing it puts you on a profound journey toward enlightenment. If you're lacking purpose and feeling lost and disconnected. Focus on spiritual growth with prayer, spiritual study, and deep meditation practices. Those will help you find meaning in life and unlock doors that trap your energetic state.

This table showcases the four main subtle bodies, how they interact with an empath's energy, and how to heal imbalances:

Subtle Body	What It Does	How Empaths Feel Imbalances	Healing Practices
Physical Body	The tangible, material body	Fatigue, body aches, feeling disconnected from the body	Yoga, nutrition, rest, movement
Emotional Body	Holds emotions, feelings, and past traumas	Feeling overwhelmed, mood swings, absorbing others' emotions	Journaling, emotional release techniques, self-love
Mental Body	Governs thoughts, beliefs, and perception	Overthinking, anxiety, self-doubt	Meditation, breathwork, reprogramming limiting beliefs
Spiritual Body	Connects to higher consciousness and intuition	Feeling lost, spiritually disconnected, lack of purpose	Prayer, spiritual study, deep meditation

EXERCISE: Subtle Body Scan:

Subtle body scans help you achieve self-awareness by identifying energy blockage. This requires breathwork and getting in touch with your inner self. It is where you peel back the layers of your energetic landscape and let energy travel down your body, connecting with the vibrations of your thoughts, feelings, and senses to understand where you need guidance.

1. Focus on each layer separately and consider how you feel. You can gain a deeper understanding of your vibrational state by asking yourself questions.
2. Scan your subtle bodies by asking yourself: "How does my physical body feel? How does my emotional body feel? How does my mental body feel? How does my spiritual body feel?"
3. When focused on a particular layer, check if you're holding onto energy that doesn't belong to you. Ask yourself questions to guide your search and determine your energy body's health.
4. **Physical body scan** – Is there tension in your physical body? Are you experiencing symptoms of fatigue and feeling disconnected from your body?
5. **Emotional body scan** – Are there negative emotions trapped within your emotional body, making you feel moody and overwhelmed with traumatic memories?
6. **Mental body scan** – Is your mental body clouded by intrusive thoughts? Are you disconnected from your spiritual body, making you feel lost?
7. **Spiritual body scan** – Is your energy confusing, making you feel spiritually disassembled and lacking purpose? Are you struggling to concentrate and connect with your consciousness?
8. Answer these questions and write down your insights.

The Chakra System

Think of the chakra system as a powerful center that stores everything your energy anatomy has ever experienced. It is an element of the spiritual subtle body with projections in the physical one. It gathers information and helps every part of your body express it.

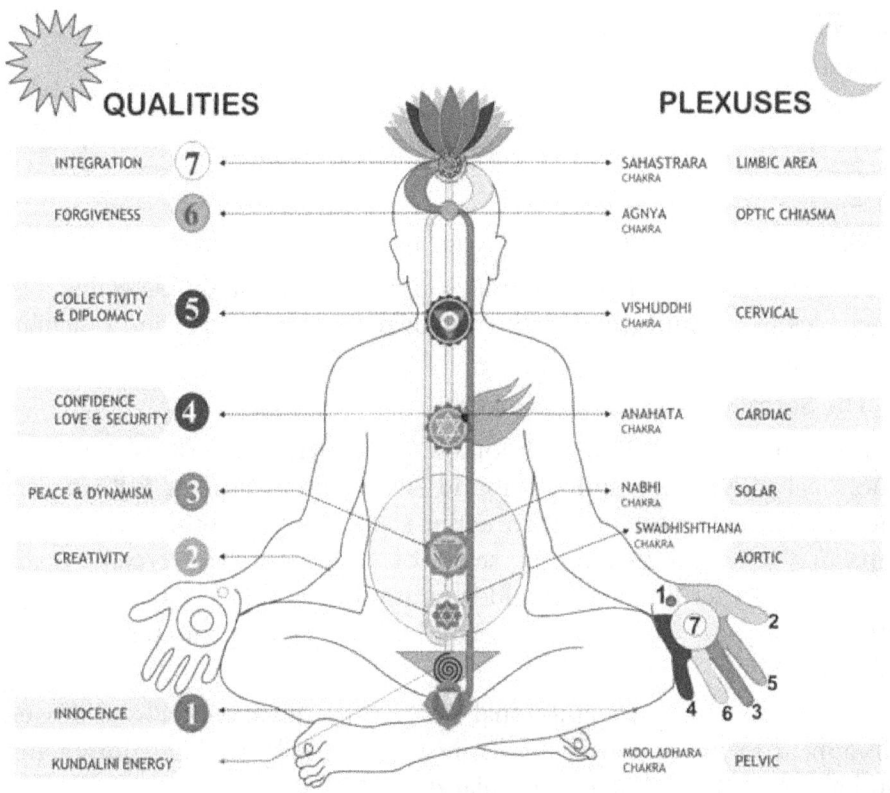

The Chakra System.[12]

This system influences your energy and is vital in improving energy flow. When your chakras are out of balance, this impacts your emotional and physical well-being and even causes tiredness or severe health problems.

Below is a more in-depth look at what the seven main chakras do and how to keep them working in tandem.

The Root Chakra (Muladhara)

The root chakra affects your pelvic floor and tailbone. A balanced Muladhara (at the base of the spine) keeps you grounded and informs you of your basic needs. It connects you to your survival instincts and sense of stability and security. It represents nature and comfort. An imbalanced root chakra represents instability.

The kidneys, bladder, large intestine, and organs close to the spine can be impacted by an imbalanced root chakra. Depression, bowel movement issues, immune system disorders, addictions, allergies, and other physical challenges can appear. The emotional issues stemming from an imbalanced Muladhara are insecurities, anxiety, and a fear of change.

Self-Assessment Questions:
1. Have you been feeling unsafe or exhausted lately?
2. Are you feeling insecure?
3. Are you struggling to keep your mind grounded?

Heal by taking a barefoot walk on the beach or grass, eating root vegetables to reconnect you with your own roots in nature, and practicing grounding meditation.

The Sacral Chakra (Swadhisthana)

Located in your lower abdomen, the sacral chakra is linked to emotional intelligence and social and sexual interaction. A fulfilling and integrated social life can improve the state of your Swadhisthana, thus impacting your sex drive, your sense of connection and creativity, and your ability to set boundaries and stay motivated. Your sexual organs are influenced by the health of the second chakra since it sits between your belly button and pubic bone.

Imbalances can cause emotional and physical problems. Physical issues will appear in the region in the form of menstrual problems, impotence, lumbar pain, and uterine or testicular diseases.

Self-Assessment Questions:
1. Do you struggle with setting boundaries?
2. Do you experience frequent mental overload?
3. Are you having difficulty processing emotions?

You can aid your lower abdomen by opening up your hips with yoga poses like the hip flexor stretch and engaging in hydrotherapy to relax your mind and open yourself up to creative expression.

The Solar Plexus Chakra (Manipura)

The solar plexus relates to organs between the chest bone and upper abdomen, such as the spleen, pancreas, stomach, liver, and gallbladder. Like these organs, the Manipura decides how well our overall health is. How you interact with the world, your capabilities, self-esteem, and career progression and success are governed by the third chakra. Ultimately, the solar plexus impacts an empath's ability to function and show up positively in life, so even stubbornness and arrogance can indicate imbalance because these are setbacks to overcome, not personality traits. Depression, low energy, and low self-esteem are other emotional signs of dysfunction. Physical signs include digestive disorders, liver cancer, and, at times, diabetes.

Self-Assessment Questions:
1. Do you feel powerless due to low self-esteem?
2. Do social interactions take away your energy and leave you feeling drained?

You can heal a dysfunctional Manipura by boosting your self-esteem with power poses and exercises like strength training, getting plenty of sun exposure, and learning to say "no" with confidence to what doesn't serve you.

The Heart Chakra (Anahata)

The heart chakra impacts empaths' ability to love and sympathize, playing a role in romance and circulation, as well as in heart and vagus nerve function. One could also be at risk of scoliosis, nervous breakdowns, and breast cancer if this chakra is left untreated. An impacted Anahata could cause issues with giving and receiving love and lead to episodes of anxiety and depression.

Self-Assessment Questions:
1. Are you currently taking on other people's pain?
2. Do you find yourself giving too much of your time and energy?
3. Are you taking on more than you can handle?
4. Do you have difficulty receiving love?

Start with changing your diet. Eat green foods to balance your chakra. Engage in heart-opening breathwork to release clogged energy, and write down self-love affirmations to repeat daily so you can rewire how you see yourself.

The Throat Chakra (Vishuddha)

The fifth chakra rules self-awareness and the ability to speak your truth. It is associated with your lungs, vagus nerve, larynx, and pharynx. Risks from an imbalance of the Vishuddha are a sore throat, asthma, and respiratory problems. You might experience shyness, suppressed emotions, paranoia, and intense introversion when out of balance.

Self-assessment questions:
1. Are you holding back emotions and keeping your thoughts to yourself too often?
2. Are you a people-pleaser and neglecting your own needs?
3. Do you fear speaking the truth about your feelings, not wanting to disappoint anyone or feel like a burden?

Be aware of how you handle interactions so unexpressed emotions won't pile up over time and lead to a blocked throat chakra (and you eventually lashing out). Singing, humming, and getting yourself out of your head can free restrictive energy. Drink herbal teas to flush out your system and heal from within.

The Third Eye Chakra (Ajna)

The third eye chakra is in the center of your forehead and rules over the ears, nose, left eye and brain. It governs an empath's ability to practice rational thinking, be insightful, and handle complex situations. If your Ajna is out of alignment, you can experience dizziness, headaches, and cataracts. Emotional issues lead to anxiety, indifference, and chronic stress.

Self-Assessment Questions:
1. Is your intuition clouded?
2. Do you struggle with anxiety and overthinking?

Combat the imbalance of the third eye through meditation, visualization, and reducing screen time.

The Crown Chakra (Sahasrara)

The crown chakra connects to the right side of your brain. Empaths are specifically affected by this chakra because it revolves around intuition. When the Sahasrara isn't aligned, you can suffer from depression, insomnia, and headaches. Emotional dysfunctions look like arrogance, pride, sadness, and even hallucinations.

Self-Assessment Questions:
1. Do you find it hard to engage with your spirit?
2. Are you struggling with a lack of direction?
3. Are you at a stage in your life where you feel lost?

The solutions to an imbalanced Sahasrara are enjoying the silence in nature, walking in a garden, spiritual study, and gratitude journaling.

This table lists the seven chakras and what causes and fixes their blockages:

Chakra	Empath-Specific Signs of Imbalance	Quick Fix
Root (Muladhara) – Base of Spine	Feeling unsafe, ungrounded, and exhausted from absorbing others' energy	Grounding meditation, walking barefoot, and eating root vegetables
Sacral (Swadhisthana) – Lower Abdomen	Emotional overload, struggling with boundaries, and difficulty processing emotions	Hip-opening yoga poses, water therapy, and creative expression
Solar Plexus (Manipura) – Upper Abdomen	Feeling powerless, drained by energy vampires, and low self-esteem	Power poses, sun exposure, and saying "no" with confidence
Heart (Anahata) – Center of Chest	Giving too much time and energy, taking on others' pain, and difficulty receiving love	Heart-opening breathwork, self-love affirmations, and green foods
Throat (Vishuddha) – Throat	Holding back emotions, people-pleasing, and fear of speaking truth	Singing, humming, and drinking herbal teas
Third Eye (Ajna) – Forehead	Overthinking, anxiety, and clouded intuition	Meditation, visualization, and reducing screen time
Crown (Sahasrara) – Top of Head	Feeling disconnected from self/spirit and lack of direction	Spiritual study, gratitude journaling, and silence in nature

Chakra Scan:

Scan your chakra with your hands by following these step-by-step instructions.

1. Close your eyes and take three slow, deep breaths through your nose and out your mouth.
2. Place your non-dominant hand in front of you, palm facing up, and use the index finger of your dominant hand to draw a spiral shape in the center of your palm. Continue this motion clockwise.
3. You should feel your hand become receptive to energy as your index finger activates it. You might feel slight pressure or a rush of heat. Some people sense flashes of light and color.
4. If you cannot feel energy activating, don't worry. It can take longer for some people. Repeat the spiral drawing in your palm exercise a few times daily until your energy sensitivity builds up.

Once you start feeling energy activate between your fingers, continue the scan to detect chakra imbalances.

1. With your non-dominant hand hovering in front of you (make sure it's four to six inches away from your body), place your dominant hand at the root chakra.
2. Hold your hand over the base of your spine for roughly ten seconds.
3. Slowly glide your hand upward, stopping at each chakra for the same amount of time until you reach the crown chakra (at the top of your head).
4. Observe how you feel at each stop and notice the change in energy from one chakra to the next.

When the scan is complete, consider the sensations you felt. Which chakra carried the most and least energy? Did you feel tingling or a spark? Write down whether some chakras gave you a sense of discomfort or weak sensations. That indicates energetic healing is required.

The Aura

The aura is the energetic field protecting you from absorbing unwanted energy, like a light shield warding off darkness. Think of it as an invisible orb that surrounds you at all times. It is an ocean of vibrations linked to reservoirs of colors, sound, and sight, gathering information and carrying it to your energy anatomy.

The aura integrates energy systems with the universe. Depending on your frequency, this dynamic shield can be a gentle and radiant presence or a storm whirring around you, protecting your vitality when unwanted energy tries to seep into your chakras. You will know your aura is strong by the sensations it brings you. You'll feel centered, less impacted by others, and exude confidence.

A weakened aura, on the other hand, struggles to function and fails to protect you from negative entities. Symptoms to look out for are exhaustion, emotional overwhelm, and if you're easily influenced by others' moods.

Practical Exercises:

These exercises strengthen your aura:

The Zip-Up Technique:

Zip up an energetic shield from your feet to the top of your head to block out negative energy.

1. Stand up straight and breathe in and out, releasing weaknesses.
2. After another inhale, place both hands in front of you, palms facing in the direction of your toes.
3. As you exhale, your hands will sweep up over the front of your body as if brushing the air from your feet to your head. Your arms should end up stretched over the crown of your head.
4. Imagine zipping up your energetic shield like a onesie.

Aura Brushing Technique

1. Sit in a comfortable position with your shoulders relaxed.
2. Focus on your intention to ward off unwanted energy. You can repeat this aloud a couple of times before you begin.
3. Cup your hands and brush them over your energy field (all around your entire body) in a circular motion, as if you're waving or shooing air away.
4. Imagine the stress attached to you being blown away.
5. Wash your hands to cleanse them of negativity.

Saltwater Bath/Shower Technique:

A saltwater bath is a great way to cleanse your aura.[18]

1. Run a bath or shower. Fill the bathtub with water, or bring a bucket into the shower with you and fill that up with water.
2. Bring a cup of salt. Use natural sea salt, Epsom salts, or pink Himalayan salt for their cleansing properties.
3. Pour the cup of salt into your bucket or bathtub and stir.
4. Pour the bucket over yourself, or dip your head under the bathtub water.
5. Water will cover your entire body from head to toe and travel down your flesh, letting good energy flow in and negative energy wash off.
6. Rinse yourself off with clear, fresh water. You will instantly feel more vibrant and positive.

Frequency

Everyone has a unique energetic frequency shaped by emotions, thoughts, and spiritual health. This puts you in a vibratory rate that fluctuates as a result of your energetic expression. High vibrational states are happy and healthy, while low vibration indicates sadness, negativity, and illness. Empaths' vibrations are sensitive and fluid, making them susceptible to external influences. They pick up on others' vibrations and mold their own to them, disrupting their energetic frequency.

Exercise:

Use this exercise to identify your baseline frequency:

1. Check-in and acknowledge where your frequency is and your baseline by asking yourself what your primary and initial feelings, thoughts, and sights are. What did you first see, think, and feel?
2. You will feel a shift as you engage with each thought and emotion. That is your baseline expanding, sharing a vibrational space with what your mind, heart, and soul perceive.
3. What fills the moment when you check in? Is it a specific experience or a dream, or are you consciously choosing what to think? Are you focused on upcoming plans or past reflections? Answering these questions helps you add a vibrational perception layer to your baseline frequency.
4. Deepen your frequency comprehension by acknowledging new sensations you become aware of. Every time you check in with yourself, you will immediately understand your emotions and what insight they provide.

This awareness will strengthen your baseline frequency. It won't be limited to your reactions. Life experiences expand your resonance, but so does practice.

Checking in with yourself not only keeps you present but also allows you to see beyond your initial perceptions. You are engaging in deep self-reflection, learning to listen to your thoughts and feelings, and improving your connection to your baseline frequency. You will learn to witness and explore other frequencies with a broad perspective, too, growing your abilities and embodying the vibrations you choose.

Frequency and Sound Healing

You can compare musical notes to your emotions.¹⁴

You can compare musical notes to your emotions to better understand frequency and establish sound healing. Think of each chakra as a musical instrument that needs to be cared for to play harmonious melodies. All these chakras belong to one orchestra, and you are their conductor, creating a symphony of energy. Each chakra is attuned to a note, which can heal your energy field.

Energy work practitioners use the 432 Hz system because of its simpler and deeper resonance with the foundational energy, but you can also use the 440 Hz standard. Both tuning standards are provided under the chakras and their attributed notes and frequencies.

- *Root Chakra*
  Musical Note: C
  Frequency: 440 tuning: 262 H / 432 tuning: 256 Hz
- *Sacral Chakra*
  Musical Note: D
  Frequency: 440 tuning: 294 Hz / 432 tuning: 288 Hz
- *Solar Plexus Chakra*
  Musical Note: E
  Frequency: 440 tuning: 330 Hz / 432 tuning: 324 Hz
- *Heart Chakra*
  Musical Note: F
  Frequency: 440 tuning: 349 Hz / 432 tuning: 342 Hz

- *Third Eye Chakra*
  Musical Note: A
  Frequency: 440 tuning: 440 Hz / 432 tuning: 432 Hz
- *Crown Chakra*
  Musical Note: B
  Frequency: 440 tuning: 494 Hz / 432 tuning: 484 Hz

Protecting and raising your frequency is essential because a low resonance can result in exhaustion, negativity, and physical illness. Apply these techniques to maintain a natural energy balance.

Meditation

Manage frequency shifts by checking in with yourself when your mind feels hectic.

1. Find a quiet, distraction-free place or garden.
2. Enjoy the silence or play the musical notes of your chakras.
3. Do breathwork to clear your mind of clutter and release unwanted energy.
4. Allow yourself to relax to protect your frequency and leave this meditative state with a stronger resolve.

Nature Walks

Take walks to reconnect with nature.[15]

Find opportunities to walk in nature daily. This will prevent negativity from attaching itself to you when your aura is weak.

1. Get sun exposure and change your route to reconnect to nature. Go to the beach, hike near the mountains, or walk in the park.
2. Breathe in fresh air, letting your energy recharge and your frequency reset.
3. By walking in nature, you are determining what your baseline frequency is – a calm state with the ability to vibrate higher.

Gratitude Exercise

Morning and evening stretches release tension that clogs your energy anatomy. Your frequency needs healthy energy flow, so your chakras must align to achieve a high vibrational state.

1. Engage in simple stretches that open up your chest and hips. Poor posture (a slouched back and hunched shoulders) does not invite good energy in.
2. As your body opens up with deep breaths mid-stretch, you'll think clearly.
3. Express what you're grateful for to return to a pure, vibrant frequency.

Positive Affirmations

Positive affirmation practices are similar to gratitude exercises.

1. Write down affirmations to rely on when negative energy clouds your beliefs. These can range from "I will take time for self-care," and "I will set clear boundaries to protect my frequency," to "My anxiety does not define me – I am returning to my healthy aura and healing my chakras."
2. Repeat until your brain believes you.

Cleanse Your Energy Field

1. Pick a way to cleanse your energy field. It can be crystals, burning incense, or listening to your chakras' music notes.
2. Set up your cleansing space by putting music on, allowing the incense's aroma to permeate, or surrounding yourself with protective crystals. Some people use all three.
3. Say your intention out loud, for example: "I am drawing positivity in and cleansing my energy field."
4. Sit in this space, take in the soothing atmosphere with each breath, and feel your unwanted essences evaporate. Your energy shield is healing, your aura is strengthening, and your energy is replenished.

Chapter 4: ENERGY WORK II: Energy Essentials and Practices for Sensitive Souls

Being an empath or a highly sensitive person means feeling things on a deeper level than most others. An empath's energy connects to people easily, and they are able to transfer and absorb vibrations to and from others around them in ways that affect them on physical, spiritual, and mental levels. In a lot of cases, these vibrations or energies are not of the favorable kind.

Because of that, some safeguards have been developed and employed over time by spiritual healers, mental health specialists, and physicians that allow HSPs to set boundaries that can protect and center their energy in a way that does not leave them constantly depleted.

Spiritual healers have worked over time to create safeguards for HSPs.[16]

There are dozens of methods used to help manage and protect energy flows in sensitive individuals. Some of these methods include things like sage smudging, healing crystals, or using essential oils. While these methods do work for many, there are four basic practices that healing professionals and practitioners have agreed upon: Grounding, breathwork, meditation, and visualization.

Those four practices are cornerstones that are often used to help empaths and non-empaths alike maintain a healthy, blockage-free energy flow and keep the soul balanced and shielded from outside negative influences.

One of the oldest principles pertaining to healing, maintaining healthy energy flows, and connecting the spiritual, mental, and physical body is the concept of chakras.

Chakra means "wheel" in ancient Sanskrit. It refers to the hundreds of spinning energy fields within and around the human body. From those hundreds, there are seven main energy centers that most healers and scholars focus on. Those centers exist parallel to the human spine and are responsible for the well-being of the person by regulating their energy flows.

These 7 chakras are:
1. Root Chakra (Muladhara)
2. Sacral Chakra (Svadhisthana)
3. Solar Plexus Chakra (Manipura)
4. Heart Chakra (Anahata)
5. Throat Chakra (Vishuddha)
6. Third Eye Chakra (Ajna)
7. Crown Chakra (Sahasrara)

Each one of these chakras is in charge of a physical and spiritual aspect of the human body. If the chakras are stable and the energy is flowing freely between them in the body, then it is expected to have a healthy and balanced emotional and physical state. On the other hand, if one of these energy centers is disturbed or blocked, the consequences may vary from mild to serious physical agony or emotional discomfort. For instance, if an empath has been absorbing the grief of others or is present for a long time in a highly stressful environment, the emotional toll caused by absorbing immense amounts of negative energy can affect several energy centers. The root (grounding and stability) and heart (emotional balance) chakras can be compromised, which can lead to an effect on the Solar plexus (digestion), as well.

Dealing with chakra imbalance employs energy cleansing methods similar to the four aforementioned ones, such as energy flow meditation to restore alignment.

Breathing techniques and chakra visualizations are also used to clear blocked energy flows and free their movement. When these techniques are coupled with grounding practices, they create a shield against intruding energy flows.

Grounding – Reconnecting with the Earth's Energy

Grounding is very much related to a person's connection to the power residing within the earth. It is basically a method that facilitates an empath's way back to it. Practicing this technique allows a person to draw on the positive energy of the earth, stabilizing their flows and decimating any negative energy stored within their body.

It facilitates the ability to be present in the current moment and anchored from any disturbing thoughts and emotions that may be pulling at your energy by utilizing the rest of the senses. These practices also have physical effects, such as reducing inflammation, increasing blood flow, and calming the nervous system. It frees the mind of distractions, allowing it to concentrate more on what needs to be done.

It can be practiced simply by walking or standing barefoot on the grass or in a water body. It can involve touching trees or holding certain Yoga poses. More complex methods involve a higher level of mindfulness. This healing method is essential in centering the root chakra, allowing the energy to flow out of the body into the earth and then back in again, cleansed and balanced.

Basic Grounding Techniques

Standing, Grounding, and Root Visualization: This exercise can be performed anywhere. Stand with your bare feet hip-width apart on the ground. Stand tall, strong, and firm. If you're unable to stand, you can sit, but make sure your feet are firmly planted on the ground. Take a deep breath, and close your eyes. Try to picture a tree in your mind's eye. See the green leaves rustling in the wind, the many branches swaying, and the strong truck reaching down to the invisible roots.

Grounding meditation.[17]

As you feel the ground below you, visualize yourself as the tree. It's your strong truck and your leaves hanging from the branches. From the soles of your feet, picture roots growing, reaching down into the earth.

Imagine the damp, dark soil beneath you. Picture yourself getting heavier, your feet sinking down into the earth, while the ground is holding you steady, unwavering, anchored.

Your roots absorb the earth's nutrients, connecting you to its strength. Your legs and waist are the trunk of the tree, tall, strong, and proud, carrying the weight of the branches and leaves upwards into the warmth of the sun.

As your breathing falls into a steady rhythm, imagine your stresses and negativity being pushed out of you with every exhale through your roots. Any tension stored in your eyes, arms, belly, or chest is absorbed by the soil. Imagine yourself getting lighter as the earth takes in everything you release.

Now, with every inhale, imagine your roots gathering light and wellness from the earth. Feel it sustain and heal your soul and body as it travels from your feet up into your trunk. You are one with the ground; it completes you. Your feet are absorbing the light and wellness from the earth and moving it up through the entirety of your body. The light fills your belly, chest, arms, and head. You are standing tall and firm while your leaves are free to move about and sway in the breeze, anchored by the roots intertwined in the soil and the rocks beneath you.

Feel the sun reaching down and touching your trunk, filling you with light. Take a moment to look at yourself and how strongly rooted and steady you are. Know without a doubt that you are able to create your own energy.

Continue to visualize this for as long as you can, and then calmly and slowly open your eyes and come back to the present. As you move away from your position, carry with you the clearing energy of the earth throughout the day.

Breathwork – Using Breath to Shift Energy and Calm the Mind

Definition and Importance

Breathing is an involuntary function that all living beings do. The respiratory center within the brain sends out signals that control the activity of the lungs. Breathing in oxygen, generating energy through cell conversion, and expelling carbon dioxide from your body with every exhale.

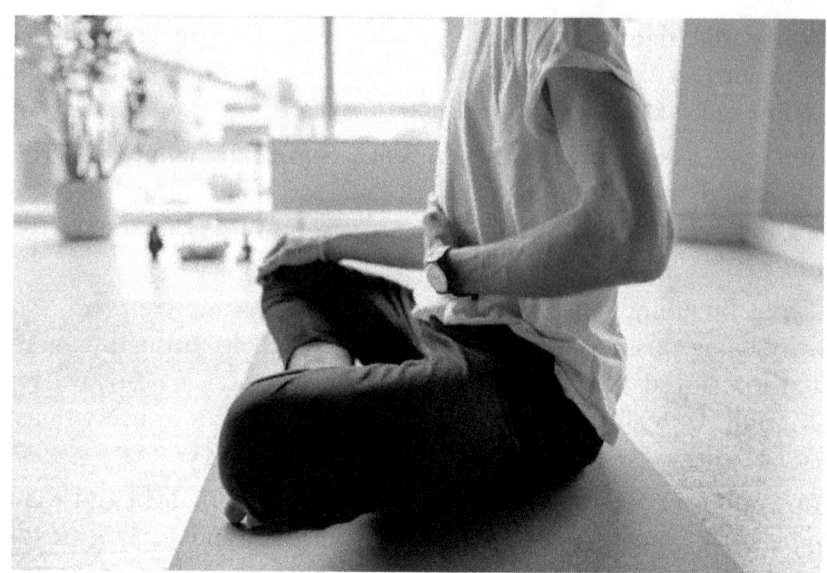
Focus on the patterns of your breathing to really get the breathwork right.[18]

The quality of the breath controls many aspects of the body and can drastically affect it in both positive and negative ways. If a person suffers from oxygen deficiency, they are at risk of developing heart problems, anxiety, fatigue, and infections. Similarly, stress can change the pattern of your breathing, which then activates the fight or flight response, which can cause shallow breathing or hyperventilation. That, in turn, can increase stress, and on and on, the cycle repeats.

Luckily, human beings can control and consciously regulate their breathing process. When an empath is in control of their breath, their energy levels can be restored to a balanced state, and their parasympathetic system is activated. The heart rate is lowered, the body is not physically compromised, and the mental state is clear and stable to deal with challenges without distractions.

Physically, stress hormones are reduced (cortisol), the immune system is powered up, and anxieties are replaced with calmness.

There are a few simple breathing exercises that, if followed regularly, can improve the energy flow levels in the body.

Simple Breathwork Techniques

Box Breathing - Also known as square breathing, this technique is favored by the Navy Seals to clear the mind and manage stress and anxiety while remaining grounded. This technique is based on an Indian form of breathwork called Pranayama.

Instructions:
1. Look for a quiet space where you can sit or lie down comfortably. While not always necessary, it's often preferred to close your eyes to center your focus completely on yourself.
2. Take a deep breath in, inhaling for four seconds.
3. Feel the sensation of the breath filling your lungs.
4. Count slowly in your head to four.
5. Imagine energy flowing into your body with each intake of breath.
6. Hold the breath in your body for another four seconds. It may feel slightly challenging at first, but it will get easier with practice.
7. Slowly exhale while counting to four.
8. Picture your negative energy, emotions, and stresses being released with the exhale.
9. Hold your breath again for four seconds. This final hold signals your body that another cycle of breath is about to begin.
10. Repeat this exercise for a few more minutes.
11. When ready, slowly open your eyes and return to the present moment.

You can adjust the length of each phase – inhale, hold, and exhale – to suit your comfort. Try to incorporate this exercise into your daily routine for better energy stabilization.

Alternate Nostril Breathing - This is another method to help calm your mind and relax the body. Scientific research suggests that each of your nostrils is directly linked to the opposite hemisphere of the brain.

It is thought that left-nostril breathing can create a sense of calmness and combat anxiety, while right-nostril breathing raises your energy levels and metabolism.

Instructions:
1. Find a comfortable seated position and close your eyes.
2. Use your thumb to close your right nostril.
3. Inhale deeply through your left nostril for 4 seconds.
4. Hold your breath.
5. Use your ring finger to close your left nostril.
6. Exhale through your right nostril for 4 seconds.

7. Inhale through your right nostril for 4 seconds.
8. Hold your breath.
9. Close your right nostril with your thumb.
10. Exhale through your left nostril for 4 seconds.
11. Continue alternating:

$$\text{Inhale left} \to \text{hold} \to \text{exhale right}$$
$$\text{Inhale right} \to \text{hold} \to \text{exhale left}$$

12. Maintain this rhythm until it feels natural.
13. If comfortable, gradually increase the inhale and exhale count.
14. Continue for a few minutes.
15. Slowly open your eyes and return to the present moment.

This practice enhances energy flow, supports the free movement of prana (life force), and balances brain activity to improve mental function.

Double Breathing - This technique raises your energy levels instantly by engaging the parasympathetic nervous system. It relieves sleepiness and brain fog. It is centered around taking short bursts of breath to rouse your energy.

Instructions:
1. Sit comfortably and close your eyes.
2. Take a short breath in through your nose, followed by a longer inhale.
3. Exhale briefly through your mouth, then follow with a longer exhale.
4. Keep your nose relaxed throughout the exercise.
5. Repeat this breathing pattern for a few minutes.
6. After every other breath, pause briefly to sense the flow of energy in your body.

When ready, slowly open your eyes and return to the present moment.

4-7-8 Breathing Technique - Also known as the relaxing breath, this technique regulates emotional outbursts such as anger and maintains control over cravings.

Instructions:

1. Sit in a comfortable position with your back straight and close your eyes.
2. Place the tip of your tongue on the roof of your mouth.
3. Exhale through your mouth, making a "whoosh" sound.
4. Close your mouth and inhale deeply through your nose while counting to 4.
5. Hold your breath for 7 seconds.
6. Exhale fully through your mouth with the "whoosh" sound while counting to 8.
7. Repeat this cycle for a few minutes.
8. As you continue, notice a growing sense of calm and presence.

When you feel ready, slowly open your eyes and return to your surroundings.

Meditation – Tuning into Your Higher Self and Universal Energy

Meditation allows you to connect with your higher self.[19]

For empaths, having a connection with their higher selves is quite essential to maintaining a steady level of energy. When a connection is lacking, energy, anxiety, and fear can take over. It would often feel like the spirit is not as connected to the body as it should be.

Definition and Importance

The higher self, also sometimes called the divine self, is basically the human extension, liberated from the ego. It is also a part of the universal higher power or cosmic energy. That energy exists within everyone. It is the connector between all beings and things.

When a person is aligned with the higher self, they have access to wisdom and information that transcends time and space. They are able to understand their purpose.

When an empath is able to establish that connection, they'll find answers to many questions they may have never thought to ask. They'll know where their strengths lie and how to use them. As the spirit and mind become in sync, energy flows become clearer and will move more freely and efficiently within you.

One of the main practices used that allows for a deeper connection to one's higher self is meditation. Meditation is a way of quieting down the mind and allowing attention to shift inward. When the mind is racing with thoughts and is unable to relax and focus, you'll find it hard to connect to your higher self. It puts a stop to that and facilitates a gateway that puts you on the path to spiritual enlightenment.

Basic Meditation Techniques

Guided Body Scan Meditation - Experts have reported that this type of meditation improves sleep, lowers anxiety levels, and can even reduce pain.

This practice can be performed by lying down or seated in a comfortable position.

Think of it as an imaginary X-ray scan of your body, from the top of your head to the tips of your toes.

Instructions:
1. Find a comfortable position and stretch out your limbs.
2. Close your eyes and bring your attention to your breath.
3. Feel the breath softly entering and leaving your lungs.
4. Shift your focus to your seated or lying position.
5. Notice how your body presses into the chair or floor.
6. Observe how the surface supports your weight.
7. Pay attention to any pressure or sensations.
8. Take a few deep breaths and bring awareness to your feet.

9. Notice the floor beneath them.
10. Sense any pulsing, vibration, pain, heat, or even the absence of sensation.
11. Move your attention to your legs.
12. Feel how they rest against the chair.
13. Observe muscle tension or heaviness.
14. Try to release any tightness.
15. Shift focus to your back.
16. Notice how it is supported by the chair.
17. Pay attention to pain, numbness, or tightness.
18. Gently relax the muscles where you can.
19. Bring attention to your stomach.
20. If it feels tight, allow it to soften.
21. Notice any discomfort or pain.
22. Focus on your arms, hands, and shoulders.
23. Relax your shoulders downward.
24. Sense any tingling, heaviness, or pulsation.
25. Move attention to your neck and throat.
26. Notice soreness or tightness.
27. Allow the muscles to soften.
28. Bring awareness to your jaw.
29. If you're clenching your teeth, release the tension.
30. Scan your face.
31. Relax your forehead and facial muscles. Notice any subtle sensations.
32. Focus on the top of your head. Sense any pressure or warmth.
33. Expand your awareness to your whole body.
34. Feel energy or vibrations moving from head to toe and back again.
35. Stay present with all sensations in your body.
36. When ready, take a deep breath and return your attention to your surroundings.
37. Slowly open your eyes and take in your environment with a soft gaze.

38. Gently move your neck from side to side.

This exercise can last anywhere from 5 to 45 minutes, based on your preference.

Heart-Centered Meditation - This energy center is situated in the middle of the breast bone, at the center of the chest. It is connected to the heart chakra, which acts as a link between the physical and spiritual chakras (top and bottom halves of your body). If this energy center is clear and in balance, it will allow you to connect easily to your surroundings, accept others unconditionally, show compassion, and love yourself.

Instructions:
1. Find a quiet place where you won't be disturbed.
2. Sit comfortably in a chair with feet on the floor or on a cushion.
3. Choose a position you can hold comfortably throughout the meditation.
4. Close your eyes and focus on your breath.
5. Observe the breath entering and exiting your body without forcing it.
6. Maintain a steady, natural rhythm.
7. Stay with your breath for a few moments.
8. If your mind wanders, gently return focus to your breath.
9. Let thoughts pass without holding onto them.
10. Try 2-3 fake yawns to trigger a real one.
11. Take a deep breath into your belly, then your chest.
12. Exhale slowly from chest to belly.
13. Repeat this twice.
14. Bring attention to the base of your spine (root chakra).
15. Visualize a red circle of energy rotating there.
16. Picture the light growing from a pin-sized dot to envelop your whole body.
17. Shift focus just below the navel (sacral chakra).
18. Visualize an orange rotating circle of energy.
19. Inhale as it grows from pin-sized to surrounding your body.
20. Move just above the belly button (solar plexus chakra).

21. Visualize a yellow rotating circle of energy growing with your breath.
22. Bring attention to your heart (heart chakra).
23. Picture a green circle of energy rotating at your chest.
24. Inhale: let the light grow to fill your heart.
25. Exhale: let it expand to surround your body.
26. Continue visualizing the green light with each breath.
27. Imagine it expressing different emotions: love, compassion, appreciation, self-love.
28. *Optional:* Use affirmations like "I am loved," "I feel grateful," and "I accept myself."
29. Spend a few minutes in silence, absorbing the energy of the light.
30. Return your focus to your breath.
31. Gently move your fingers and toes and shift your limbs.

When ready, open your eyes slowly, starting with a soft gaze.

Visualization – Using the Mind's Eye to Clear Energy and Manifest Protection

Healing through visualization is one of the most effective methods used to regenerate and mend energy flows within sensitive people. But what is visualization? To understand it, an examination of intent is crucial first.

Definition and Importance

Intent is the focused thoughts and energy moving in a specific direction to reach a certain goal. Visualization is picturing circumstances in one's mind that align with the intent. Basically, Visualization is the road that the intent takes to reach the subconscious mind.

In some instances, visualization has been proven to positively affect the physical body. Whether that's reducing stress hormones before a surgical procedure, increasing the ability to navigate pain, or controlling cravings.

There is no one way to use this tool, and not all types of visualizations can have the same effect. There are three modes that people use to visualize:

1. **Tactile:** Picturing how the energy feels.
2. **Visual:** Seeing the shape or color of the energy and its movements.
3. **Auditory:** Hearing its sound.

These three modes can be used individually, in pairs, or all together, depending on the person's preference and what works best for them.

In the exercises below, you will employ these modes in different ways that will help you ascertain which one works for you.

Guided Visualizations

Energy Clearing Visualization

Instructions:

1. Sit on the floor with your back supported against a wall.
2. Close your eyes and take a few deep, comfortable breaths.
3. Visualize a ball of positive, inviting light above your head.
4. Imagine the energy flowing down and around your body.
5. See it entering the top of your head like a waterfall.
6. Feel it moving through your spine and limbs.
7. Picture it gathering negative thoughts and emotions, pushing them down and out into the ground.
8. Take your time allowing all negative energy to be cleared.
9. Feel it transform into light, positive energy.
10. Once you feel lighter and clearer, visualize a second ball of light above your head.
11. Choose a color that represents gratitude to you.
12. Let this light enter and fill your entire body.
13. Savor the emotions and sensations it brings.
14. When you're ready, visualize a third ball of bright white light above your head.
15. Imagine it circling around your body, sealing in the positive energy.
16. Take a moment to thank Mother Earth for the renewed, pure energy.
17. Take a few more deep breaths.
18. Slowly open your eyes and return to the present moment.

Protective Shield Visualization - This visualization will allow you to create protective armor around your energy that not only keeps out unwanted and negative energies but also attracts and brings in positive ones.

Instructions:
1. Take a few deep breaths, focusing on the movement of your chest.
2. Visualize yourself standing in the center of a glimmering bright white light.
3. See it clearly around you, knowing it's present.
4. With each inhale, imagine drawing the light into your body.
5. Feel its purity filling you.
6. With each exhale, picture the light wrapping around you and settling near your feet.
7. Continue breathing:
8. Inhale the light into your body.
9. Exhale it around you, layering it over previous exhales.
10. Build the light layer by layer until it completely surrounds you.
11. Focus on thickening the light around your heart and head for added protection.
12. Visualize the light growing firmer and denser with every breath, forming an impenetrable shield.
13. Within this shield, feel safe, happy, centered – and protected from all negativity. Only love, healing, and light can reach you.
14. When you feel complete, take a few final deep breaths.

Open your eyes, holding the certainty that your shield is secure and nothing negative can penetrate it.

Manifestation Visualization - A lot of people use visualization as a tool to manifest favorable outcomes. Manifestation is rooted in the belief that you can use your thoughts and energy to shape your reality, bringing your dreams and goals to life.

Doing that involves setting clear intentions of what you want, picturing the outcome, keeping a positive head state, and taking actionable steps towards that goal.

Before you start, you need to be clear about what you're manifesting. You need to be detailed in the outcome you're looking for. If it's financial welfare, to what extent? If it's a new house, what will it look like? A new job, what will you do?

In the case of an empath, it can be better emotional balance or stable energy management. You can picture how you'll feel and function once you've achieved them.

You need to also focus on the positives that will come out of said manifestation. This is essential to stay motivated. The more details you include, the easier it is for your mind's eye to start taking action.

Instructions:
1. Close your eyes and take a few deep breaths.
2. Visualize yourself at the finish line – you've achieved your goal.
3. Picture the exact situation you want to be in.
4. Engage all your senses: What do you see, hear, smell, feel, and taste?
5. Feel the joy and satisfaction of finally being there.
6. Add vivid details to make the scene feel real, but stay centered and calm.
7. Focus on positive emotions like gratitude, happiness, and determination.
8. If negative thoughts arise, take a few deep breaths to quiet them.
9. Acknowledge them without judgment and return gently to your vision.
10. Be compassionate with yourself throughout the process.

Practice this visualization daily for 5 minutes, imagining yourself already living your desired outcome.

Combining Practices – Creating a Daily Energy Work Ritual

Once a level of familiarity has been established with each of the exercises, you can start mixing and matching techniques in a way that best suits you and achieves the most effective outcome.

You can create your own personalized daily energy-preserving routine that keeps you centered, protected, and confident in your own skin.

Sample Ritual

- Begin with grounding yourself. Take a few deep breaths, close your eyes, and picture yourself standing tall in a yard. Your feet are bare, and from their soles, roots are growing and extending into the ground beneath you. The roots connect you to Mother Earth and draw on its positive energy while draining the negative emotions from you. Spend five minutes picturing the process as it cleanses you.
- Now, shift your attention to your breath, take a deep inhale for 4 seconds, hold the breath for another 4, and release in 4 seconds; repeat the breathwork for 5 more minutes to keep your mind focused and clear of any interrupting thoughts.
- After that, start observing your body. From the soles of your feet to the top of your head. Go body part by body part, noticing any sensations, feelings, or tensions in the muscles. Relax your muscles bit by bit until you reach the top of your head. Spend 10 minutes observing and noticing how you feel within your body.
- In the end, visualize a ball of light at the top of your head, moving in, clearing out any residual negative thoughts or emotions left, and pushing it out through the roots that grew from your feet. Imagine the light encircling you and sealing the outline of your body. The light then moves to build around you a protective, impenetrable shield of invisible light that gets stronger with every intake and exhale of breath.

You can customize your daily ritual however you want, using any combination of the techniques. Make sure to maintain a routine for at least 21 days to build a healthy habit that will help you manage and clear your energy flows and protect your emotional and spiritual welfare.

Chapter 5: SPIRITUAL DEFENSE I: Recognize and Release the Negative and Toxic

As an empath, you function as an energetic sponge. Without even trying, you tend to absorb the energy, emotions, and intentions of the people around you. While this helps you connect on a deeper level with others and the world at large, it can also make you vulnerable to negative and toxic influences. In this chapter, you'll explore the crucial aspects of learning to recognize and release the negative energy that might infect you. This is the first essential step in building a strong spiritual defense.

Learn to recognize and release negative energy.[30]

What Is Negative Energy?

This might be a term you hear and encounter often. It can also sometimes be used in a more casual way of simply referring to unpleasant ideas or people around you. For empaths, though, it can mean something entirely different.

Negative energy isn't just about being in a bad mood or bad luck. It's a residue of energy that weighs you down. It can cloud your judgment and drain your spirit very quickly. It shows up in toxic environments. These are the places where a conflict in your life or some suffering that may have happened to you lingers. It could even be places that create an enormous amount of stress in you. For example, a tense office where expectations are too high, a hospital ward where something triggering happened to you, or even a home full of unspoken resentment.

Another form that negative energy takes is toxic people. Remember, this isn't referring to people who are necessarily "bad." These are just people in your life who thrive on drama, creating issues out of nothing, poking holes in an already fraying rope, and just generally being problematic. The people who take their strength from manipulating others or controlling them. Being surrounded by those who may gaslight you or try to mold your thoughts and actions to fit their life instead of yours can truly flood your spirit with this negativity and consistently drain your energy.

Negative energy doesn't necessarily come from places you expect. Sometimes, it's simply from emotional leftovers. As an empath, you likely often pick up on emotional energy that doesn't even belong to you. Whether it's a stranger's grief, a co-worker's anxiety, or a friend's anger, you absorb this 'negative' emotional energy into your own spirit. Now, this isn't necessarily anyone's fault. However, it's important to be aware of this and learn how you can navigate this time of emotional overspill.

For empaths, this negative energy isn't just unpleasant. It can be very personal. It sticks to you and seeps into your spirit. That's because your energetic field is more open and sensitive than most. Instead of just noticing the energy, your body may take it on, storing it in your emotions and thoughts. Over time, it can lead you to chronic exhaustion, emotional instability, or even physical illness if not released.

Recognizing Negative Energy

Before you can release or protect yourself from negative energy, you need to learn how to spot it.

Toxic People and Relationships

Empaths naturally seek to help and heal others, so you often find yourself in one-sided relationships where you give far more than you receive. This dynamic is quite common for empaths and is deeply draining.

Toxic relationships can slowly deteriorate your well-being.[31]

Being around toxic people as an empath doesn't only bother you. It affects you deeply. You may absorb their anger or sadness as if it were your own. After spending time with them, you might feel heavy or emotionally cluttered. You can become uncharacteristically irritable or anxious. In extreme cases, you may even start to question your own feelings and reality.

Being in a toxic relationship, whether it's romantic, familial, platonic, or professional, can feel like walking through emotional quicksand. You may feel responsible for these people's emotions and their emotional turmoil. Maybe you can't even tell you're doing this, but the effects are there. Your fatigue and energy-draining are real and valid.

But how can you tell if a relationship is toxic?

Some signs of toxicity in relationships include:

- You feel emotionally exhausted after spending time with the person.
- You constantly feel the need to "fix" or save them.
- They consistently invalidate your feelings or try to manipulate you to feel a certain way (usually through gaslighting you).
- You feel guilty any time you set boundaries for yourself or even say "no."
- They make you feel like you need to walk on eggshells around them because there are no guarantees of how they'll act or react to you.
- They constantly criticize you in everything you do, making you think that you are lesser or incapable of successfully doing anything. This undermining of your efforts is a major factor in increasing Imposter Syndrome among empaths.
- You generally don't feel any empathy or emotional support from them. It's a one-sided exchange. You give. They take.
- Your intuition is telling you something is off, even if they appear charming or "nice."

Those are some of the many red flags that empaths like you can take note of and realize the toxicity and negative energy that person is bringing to your life. Another example is if you feel heavy or anxious every time you walk away from or leave someone, they may be a source of negative energy. This isn't to say that any interaction that makes you feel down or confused is automatically one steeped in negative energy. It's important to try to discern between consistent toxicity and simply a loved one having an off day.

The Energetic Imprint of Environments

As you know, spaces hold energy. Have you ever walked into a room and immediately felt tension in the air even though no one was speaking? Or entered a quiet, natural spot and instantly felt lighter?

Being an empath means you feel this strongly. Some environments – like hospitals, nursing homes, and crowded public transport – almost hum with this heaviness. This can also include offices or workplaces full of stress and conflict, even if it doesn't affect you directly. Even places like thrift stores or antique shops can carry residual energy from previous owners.

You may pick up on the lingering vibes of a space even if others don't seem to notice anything. You might feel physically affected or emotionally overwhelmed without an obvious cause. You need to accept that this isn't your imagination. Your sensitivity helps you detect what others usually miss. Without the right tools and techniques, these imprints can build up and weigh you down.

How to Audit Your Energy

To better understand how negative energy is showing up in your life, here's a simple reflection exercise. You'll need a quiet space, a journal or notebook, and a few minutes of uninterrupted time.

Find a quiet space to journal.[22]

1. Take a moment to evaluate and filter through the energies surrounding you.
2. Make a list of environments or people that consistently leave you feeling drained, anxious, numb, or even physically sick (such as headaches, tension, nausea, etc.). Be honest with yourself.
3. Don't judge yourself for your reactions or your feelings. This is about awareness, not blame. Even if the list includes coworkers, friends, or family members who always need emotional support but offer none in return, your reaction is valid. The list might also have specific places like rooms in your childhood home that feel chaotic or nonphysical spaces like a certain social media platform.

4. Write down the physical or emotional sensations you experience interacting with these people or being in those places.
5. Think about exactly what happens in your body when you're around this person or place. Are there any changes in your mood or thoughts? How long does it take you to feel like yourself again after the experience? Is there anything that helps you recover?
6. Once you've reflected, take a deeper look at your list. You might notice patterns of certain types of people or environments affecting you more than others. You might even recognize specific emotional triggers. As a first stage, simply being aware of these patterns can help you reclaim your power.

Understanding Energy Vampires

If you're an empath, you've likely walked away from a conversation or an interaction feeling inexplicably tired or emotionally foggy. You probably entered the situation feeling upbeat and grounded, but before you knew it, that inner light in you dimmed. That's often the effect of an energy vampire.

What Is an Energy Vampire?

You've definitely met energy vampires before, even if you didn't realize it. An energy vampire is someone who unconsciously (or sometimes, on purpose) feeds off the emotional and energetic life force of others. This especially happens to empaths. Now, these "vampires" aren't always malicious. Oftentimes, they're simply unaware of the effect they have on you. There are many types of energy vampires that you might encounter in your life:

- **The Drama Magnet:** This person is always in crisis. They have a way of turning even the smallest hiccups into massive issues. They feed on the emotional intensity of situations, and the more people involved, the better. Their lives are chaotic, and they expect you to 'fix' it or at least drop everything to help them.

- **The Constant Complainer:** This person sees the world through a lens of negativity and pessimism. They rarely look for solutions and can create a problem out of thin air. All they really want is validation for the misery they are feeling (and occasionally, for everyone else to share in that misery as well).

- **The Manipulator:** They use guilt, control, gaslighting, passive-aggression, or victimization to get what they want. In most situations, they will never be at fault or take the blame for anything.
- **The Narcissist:** They need attention and admiration constantly. Their emotional needs come before anyone else's, and they rarely empathize in return.
- **The Martyr:** They make you feel guilty for setting boundaries. They see themselves as the ones who "do everything for everyone" and will never let you forget it.
- **The Over-Sharer:** They're the ones who dump their emotional baggage onto you without asking. Since empaths tend to put others' needs above their own, you don't try to stop this person or reinforce your boundaries with them.
- **The Chronic Interrupter:** This person never listens to your thoughts or emotions and dominates every conversation. They believe that whatever they need to say takes priority over anyone else's words.

These people usually don't mean to harm. They're simply coping with their own unhealed wounds, unmet needs, and unresolved trauma. Their presence can still take a serious toll on you.

Why Are Empaths Drawn to Them?

It's the painful truth, and since you're an empath, you are probably usually a magnet for energy vampires. This is because you feel other people's pain and want to help. You are deeply compassionate and intuitive. You naturally pick up on others' feelings, even without trying. Therefore, for those struggling or seeking validation themselves, you're a safety net.

Energy vampires are drawn to generous and compassionate people. You're someone who listens to them, gives freely from your energy, and takes others' pain as your own. You are ideal.

You might even struggle with setting boundaries because you want to be open and available for others, but this will make you vulnerable to emotional overextension. Empaths also have this innate desire to heal and comfort. You may feel that if you just love someone hard enough, you can help them change or feel better. While your intentions are commendable, you can't fix an energy vampire by kindness alone. You shouldn't have to sacrifice your own well-being in the name of empathy.

Over time, these relationships can lead to burnout and resentment of those people. This is especially saddening when these people might not intend to be energy vampires and don't realize how they're negatively affecting your energy.

Identify Your Vampires

Find a quiet space where you can relax for a few minutes. When you're ready, grab a journal and write down the names of people you interact with regularly, from friends, family, co-workers, and acquaintances. Next to each name, answer the following questions:

- How do you feel before you spend time with this person?
- How do you feel after you've interacted with them?
- Do you feel depleted, anxious, or overwhelmed afterward?
- Do you feel energized or supported?
- Do you feel like you have to "shrink" yourself?
- Do you find yourself trying to "fix" their problems?
- Do you feel emotionally manipulated, like your feelings were invalidated and forced to change?
- Do they make you feel guilty for having needs?

You're not labeling anyone as "good" or "bad" here. You're simply recognizing which relationships nourish you and which don't. Again, you'll notice patterns – one person who always calls you to vent but never asks how you're doing or one who demands time but never gives you theirs.

Releasing and Clearing Negative Energy

While recognizing the negative energy is vital, the real power emerges when you learn how to release it.

Mind-Body-Energy Connection

When your energy field is overloaded, it might show up in the body. Empaths can experience fatigue, headaches or migraines, insomnia or nightmares, digestive issues, tightness in the chest or throat, and other symptoms. These are physical manifestations of the surge of negative energy taking root in your body.

Releasing Techniques

Breathwork: This includes deep belly breathing with the intention to move the energy in the body. Imagine each breath sweeping your body clean.

Salt baths: Salt is naturally purifying. A bath with Epsom or sea salt can draw out negative energy.

Nature Walks: By spending time barefoot in nature, you help your body discharge all the excess energy back into the Earth.

Shake It Off: Movement can release stagnant energy. Dancing, stretching, jumping around, and shaking out your hands, arms, and legs keep the energy moving in your body.

Emotional and Energetic Boundaries

This is an area where many empaths struggle, so don't be discouraged. Setting boundaries doesn't mean you're selfish. It means you value your well-being. You should start small, like practicing saying no without apologizing. Do not feel guilty. Saying 'no' isn't a rejection but self-respect. Or limit the time you spend with draining people – you can even schedule recovery time after those interactions. You don't have to engage in every conflict around you or solve every emotional crisis. Visualize a "no entry" sign at the edge of your aura and expect people to respect it. If toxic people or energy vampires feel the slightest hesitation in your resolve or shake in the boundary, they will trample all over it and take advantage of your emotional availability.

Cleansing Tools

- **Sage**: Burning sage (also called smudging) has been used for centuries to clear negative energy. Burn it with intention, and let the smoke purify your aura and environment.

Smudging removes negative energy.[28]

- **Palo Santo:** This sacred wood has a sweet aroma that calms the spirit and works like sage to pass the energy through your body.
- **Sound Healing:** Use bells, singing bowls, or even chanting to shift energetic patterns.
- **Visualization:** Picture a waterfall or white light washing over you, cleansing you completely. The power of your imagination and your mind's eye cannot be overstated.

Aura Smoke Cleanse

Light a piece of sage or incense, then gently blow it out. As the smoke rises, stand in a quiet space. Slowly pass the smoke around your body, over your head, and down your arms, torso, legs, and feet. Visualize the smoke pulling out the sticky, dark energy from your aura. Say out loud:

"I release all energy that is not mine. I call back my power and fill the space with light."

With the clearing of the smoke, feel the shift in your energy. Imagine the darkness of the smoke dispersing in the air as the negative energy leaves your body and returns to the universe.

Chakra Shower Meditation

Instructions:

1. Find a quiet place to sit or lie down. This exercise is perfect right before bed, especially after a long day.
2. Picture a stream of energy moving from the top of your head to the base of your spine. This is your chakra line.
3. Visualize each chakra as a spinning ball of light:
   - Red (root) at your tailbone.
   - Orange (sacral) below your navel.
   - Yellow (solar plexus) at your stomach.
   - Green (heart) at your chest.
   - Blue (throat) at your neck.
   - Indigo (third eye) at your forehead.
   - Violet or white (crown) at the top of your head.
4. As you move through each chakra, it is cleansed and brightened.
5. When you reach the base, picture a beam of white light flowing over you like a gentle shower.
6. Stay in this space as long as you need to feel the negative energy in your body being replaced by the pure light of your own spirit.

Energetic Cord Cutting

While there are plenty of healthy connections you form, there are still those that drain you. Close your eyes and visualize any cords connecting you to people or situations that feel heavy. With love, imagine cutting these cords, saying,

"I release this connection and call all my energy back to me."

Your energy can now return to your body with no shame or regret.

Energy Protection and Defense Strategies

Now that you've learned how to recognize and clear the negativity, it's time to strengthen your energetic defenses.

Grounding Techniques

One of the most important steps in spiritual defense is grounding – the process of connecting your energy to the Earth. When you're grounded, you're stable and less likely to be swept away by the emotional currents around you. You're anchoring your energy into something steady. Grounding is a great way to stay present in the moment and remain connected. This stabilizes your energy and the field with which you surround yourself.

Try standing barefoot on grass or soil while practicing grounding meditations, such as picturing roots growing from your feet. These roots can then spread wide and far, drinking in energy that nourishes you. Moreover, you can sit quietly and hold a grounding stone like hematite or red jasper. Eating certain foods like root vegetables and warm soups also helps in grounding you.

Breathwork is another powerful grounding technique. Inhale slowly through your nose for four counts, hold for four, exhale through your mouth for four, and hold again for four. Repeat this cycle as long as you need to calm your spirit and become more centered with each breath.

Protective Crystals

Crystals are a good choice for empaths because they act like armor for your energy. These include black tourmaline, which absorbs and transmutes negative energy; obsidian, which shields your spirit and detoxifies it; and amethyst, which calms the mind and strengthens your intuition.

Crystals can protect you from negative energy.[34]

Symbols of Protections

Remember that wearing or visualizing protection symbols can reinforce your auric shield. You can use the Hamsa, the open hand symbol that's believed by many cultures around the world to ward off evil and negativity. There is also the Pentagram, which combines protection with elemental balance in your spirit. Other ancient protective icons include the Ankh and the Eye of Horus, both of which call upon energies beyond your body to infuse your spirit with strength and life-giving forces.

You can draw these symbols on paper or wear them as jewelry, carrying them with you.

Auric Shields

Your aura is the energy field surrounding your body. When your aura is strong, it serves as a natural barrier against outside energies. When it's weaker, you may feel drained or overwhelmed. One way to strengthen it is to practice visualizing an auric shield. This is a simple yet powerful technique where you imagine a glowing field of light surrounding your body. As you breathe in, the light becomes brighter and denser, then as you breathe out, it expands around you.

Detoxing Practices

Protecting your energy also involves releasing what you've already absorbed. Detoxing, both spiritually and physically, realigns your energy with your true self. Hydration is the most accessible way to keep your energy flowing. Drinking plenty of water helps flush toxins and unmoving energy from you. Herbal teas, like nettle, dandelion, lemongrass, and chamomile, also work to cleanse your system.

Furthermore, there are energy healing practices, like Reiki, Qi Gong, and yoga, that can release negativity and restore your spirit. These help activate your body's natural healing flow and process emotions that may be stuck.

Creating a Bubble of Light
Instructions:
1. Close your eyes and breathe deeply.
2. Visualize a glowing bubble of light forming around your body. It can be any color you choose.
3. Imagine its edges hardening to be impenetrable to negativity. However, it remains permeable to love and light. Repeat this mantra:

"I am safe. I am protected. Only love and truth may enter my space."

Keep this shield with you all day, always pictured in your mind as you go about your life. The image in your head will reflect on the way you allow people into your energy field and how you let their energy either bounce off your bubble or through the light.

Crystal Armor
Instructions:
1. Hold your chosen crystal in your hand and close your eyes.
2. Visualize its energy forming an armor or field around your body.
3. Let it settle around your heart.
4. Carry the crystal with you throughout the day, acting as a point of origin and grounding for your energy.
5. As long as you have the crystal, the visualization of your protective armor can be stronger and clearer. At the end of the day, you can place it under your pillow for energetic support while you sleep.

As an empath, you were born with the gift of deep emotional connection and insight, but your sensitivity needs protection. Recognizing and releasing negative energy is the first step. By honoring your energy, setting clear boundaries, and using protective tools and techniques, defend your energy instead of being a victim of it.

Chapter 6: SPIRITUAL DEFENSE II: Recover from Negative Energy Drains and Attachments

As an empath learns to navigate, detect, and release energy flows, they may notice that the healing process is very slow. This is due to the fact that not all energies experienced by empaths roll off easily; some of them latch on for a while. It may take some time to fully recover and heal from those negative influences, which are also known as energy attachments.

Pay attention to people and surroundings that drain you of your energy.[25]

These attachments tend to connect to the empath's subtle body, ego, subconscious, memories, and mind. It is thought that human beings are made up of several layers of vibrating energy. Each one vibrates in a certain way and serves a specific purpose. When an empath interacts with intruding energies, these energies tend to pass through their physical form and latch onto their essence.

Throughout this chapter, you will examine how to recognize these attachments, how they come about, their effects, and how to deal with and recover from them.

Recognizing Energy Drains

Energy drain commonly occurs from interactions with specific people. They often manifest as a sense of unexplained foreboding or exhaustion when in a specific place.

Multiple factors can be responsible for energy drainage. Each situation can cause a different symptom or reaction within the body and mind. Should someone find themselves in the same situation again, pinpointing these reasons and identifying them would help manage them later.

Social Media: The constant and regular access to others in this day and age has been an astounding accomplishment. However, this advancement comes at a price. It's only reasonable to assume that most people on social platforms paint themselves in the best light in front of their followers.

Social media can slowly but surely drain you of your focus and energy.[26]

This kind of content often fosters a sense of comparison between yourself and the creator. It could develop a sense of shame in one's accomplishments, viewing them in a lesser light. People often start comparing their personal appearance to that of celebrities, ignoring the fact that, more often than not, these icons always have help. For an empath, this can take a deeper toll, leaving them reeling from electronic influence longer than less sensitive people.

Empaths can suffer from energy drains after posting stories of their own. Spending so much time picking the right filter or music to make it perfect enough for what other people are doing online.

Because social media is quite addictive, without proper self-control, overexposure can leave an empath tired for most of the day. It can take some time to train yourself to stop always reaching for your phone, but the improved emotional and mental state is definitely worth it.

Narcissistic Personalities: Nowadays, people feel more comfortable discussing mental health disorders and therapy. With that in mind, awareness of this disorder has definitely risen. Narcissism can range from a little bit of self-centeredness to fully diagnosed psychopaths and toxic narcissists. Because of the manipulative nature of this disorder, it is sometimes hard for people to spot a narcissist right away.

For empaths, they can often find themselves entangled with these personalities after mistaking the need for control and attention for having a deep connection. Having a sensitive personality, unfortunately, makes you a target of narcissists and energy vampires simply because it makes you easier to control. It takes a while to break free from a relationship like this. Narcissists often fight to maintain their supply of energy and control their surroundings.

Being around these types of people for long periods can continuously drain an empath's energy. The effect can also last when the narcissist is not around since they can assert their presence through other means in the digital age.

The negative effects sustained from being around these people can last quite a while, even after breaking free. Since they tend to make people question themselves, it can take some time to completely sever the connection and regain control over one's energy flow. It is always important to take a step back and evaluate the people you deal with at the first sign of discomfort to be able to shield yourself from unwanted influences. Setting boundaries and even going completely radio silent with them can be necessary at times to protect oneself.

Conflict: Most people can tell when a fight has just broken out in a room. The signs are usually unmistakable. For an empath, they go a little further than just noticing tension. They take that tension on and absorb it into themselves, fully experiencing the emotions and negative vibrations. Sometimes, they can even pick up on subtle tensions that others don't notice. This alertness can be exhausting and leave them confused about why they feel drained.

It's a good idea to leave at the first sign of confining energy before being immersed in it. In situations like this, empaths start experiencing feelings of irritability. An appropriate notion to consider in these circumstances can be summed up in the saying, "Not my circus, not my monkeys." One person can't fix everything, but they can save their emotional health from the trouble and effects of conflicts that don't involve them.

Dishonesty: Some people refer to empaths as "human lie detectors." The reason behind that may lie with their otherworldly abilities, such as clairvoyance and claircognizance. This type of intuition is very common with empaths. Scientifically, it may not make sense, but that doesn't mean you shouldn't trust it.

When an empath is constantly around a dishonest person, this companionship can easily drain their energy and keep them triggered. The drain can manifest in a feeling of exhaustion or anger. If this intuition repeats itself around a certain individual, keeping a safe distance from them may be best. This will safeguard against unnecessary strains on the energy.

Planetary Shifts: Empaths have a deep connection to the Earth. It heals them, and they use it to restore their balance and energy flow levels. It only stands to reason then that when the earth suffers, empaths can feel it. Earthquakes, tsunamis, fires, and other natural calamities can affect empaths to a certain level.

Intuitive people tend to feel the effects and pains of the earth rippling within their energy. Every now and then, try to practice grounding yourself and use healing exercises to recharge your energy so you're not constantly in a depleted state.

Energy Attachments

Several types of energy attachments can form between people, environments, and experiences. There are two main types: cords and hooks.

Cords of Attachments: Also called ethereal or etheric cords. These cords are present in all human beings and exist at a subconscious and unconscious level. They are basically energy-based connective lines joining two people together. Each person has one cord connecting them to another. They are responsible for transmitting information, emotions, and energy between two souls.

As an empath interacts with people, they are continuously creating new cords. These cords can be a product of love, causing no ill effects, but at times, they can be the result of negative emotions like fear and manipulation. Cords exist in two categories: minor and major. Every person has quite a few in every category, depending on their social status and the significance of the people, events, or places connected to that cord.

These connections are mostly invisible. However, some people, through a practice focused on envisioning and seeing auras and chakras, can eventually see the cords.

Most people, however, can feel the cords. Depending on the place where the cord is connected, you may feel pain, heat, inspiration, or any other sensation depending on the relationship that struck the cord. Cords only exist when permission is given, whether consciously or subconsciously, to form.

A person can have a cord of attachments with not only the living but also the people they love who have moved on from this life. These cords can also exist with other entities known as spirit guides.

With positive energy cords, a balance usually exists in the energy exchange. This energy is mostly loving and caring. When one party needs positive energy from the other, it is given (and vice versa) in equal measure. The natural possible exception to that is between a parent and a child, where the parent often gives the child more positive energy than they receive back.

Conversely, negative cords of attachments usually deplete your positive energy, leaving you high and dry. This occurrence doesn't always happen on purpose. In some cases, people may do it subconsciously due to their dependence on the attachment, not knowing that they are causing harm.

Hooks: Others would be able to hook into another's energy only when the latter party allows it to happen. This happens often when the first party says things that negatively affect the other's emotions. People use hooks to strip power away from others. Empaths are often easy targets because they are easily guilted into sympathizing with others. These hooks allow the offending party to siphon energy and leave their victims feeling drained or even sick and unable to move on from them.

To be able to remove a person's hook, they need to acknowledge that, on some level, they have allowed them to take their power. That can happen if the empath believes they need the other person's approval or endorsement in some way. It can also happen if they are trying to "fix" someone, believing in their ability to rescue them. This is also common with people pleasers. Unless control is taken back and the initial permission for them to insert the hook is revoked, they'll keep finding ways to come back and drain the remaining energy.

Symptoms to Watch Out For

Negative Expectations	You feel dread at the thought of meeting someone or being in close proximity to them.
Overthinking	You replay past interactions with certain people to the point of exhaustion and frustration.
Emotional and Mental Fog	You feel plagued with negative and overwhelming emotions, like fear and doubt. Your intuition doesn't feel as sharp as usual. You may feel hopeless or defeated.
Indifference	You feel a sense of separation or detachment when speaking to certain individuals. You may also feel a sense of detachment from your own purpose or happiness.
Sleep Troubles	You have nightmares, or trouble falling asleep, or you wake up tired.
Physical Impact	You are suddenly tired and depleted after your social interaction, which can extend to falling ill. It may also turn into a chronic condition where you're always tired. A lot of the time, the discomfort shows up as head troubles or an imbalance in the heart chakra.
Cancellation Euphoria	You are relieved when plans with someone are canceled, and you no longer have to see them. There is a sense that they pull you down.

How Attachments Form

Emotional Ties: Emotional ties, or attachments, refer to the feeling of closeness or intimacy towards another person, place, or event. These attachments are a key ingredient in forming human connections. The first ones people experience are usually with their parents or caregivers. These bonds, formed early on in a child's life (referred to by psychologists as attachment theory), foster the manner in which a person interacts and connects with future friends and loved ones.

Attachments aren't necessarily of a sexual or romantic nature. They can be just a sense of ease, safety, and comfort towards one another. However, there is more than one type of emotional attachment, and not all of them are positive.

Four main types sum up the majority of emotional ties:

1. **Secure Attachment** - This type is one of the most common in society today. It is estimated that around 60% of attachments can be categorized as secure. This type of tie is formed when there is a sense of confidence and ease within a relationship. It allows for trust to exist between the two parties. Emotional support and needs will be met, too.

   This type of attachment is built on the foundation of how each person experienced emotional connections as a child. When children grow up trusting their parents or caregivers to support and protect them emotionally and physically, they carry this sensation into their future interactions, as well.

   With insecure attachments, if a child experiences negative forms of bonds that may have developed out of fear, they could grow up having trouble bonding and trusting others. They would suffer from a lot of unresolved anger and may seek any means to maintain control of their surroundings. It can also keep them stuck in toxic relationships out of fear of being alone. Insecure relationships are not life sentences. They can transform into positive ones through perseverance, treatment, and healing.

2. **Anxious Attachment** - Also known as preoccupied attachment, this type of tie exists when a person is suffering from a negative self-image. In some cases, they idolize the other party, viewing them as better or superior to them. This type of behavior often causes anxiety due to their fear that their partner may deem them

unworthy at some point, and they would end up alone and abandoned.

This type of attachment is considered similar to insecure attachment. One of its most common symptoms is neediness and clingy behavior.

At times, this behavior can stem from childhood connections to an unpredictable caregiver, leaving their child wondering if they will be around for them or not and in constant fear of being abandoned.

3. **Avoidant Attachment** - This tie is another form of insecure attachment. This type usually stems from negligent parents or caregivers who usually put a child's needs at the bottom of their priorities. As a result, the child grows up with the conviction that they should only rely on themselves and are often uncomfortable with dependence and intimacy.

   These people often feel that being in a relationship with others is not essential to their self-worth. They often suppress their emotions during conflicts and feel the need to step back if they sense the other person is relying on them more.

   By doing so, the person experiencing this type of attachment may leave the other partner questioning their value and feeling rejected.

4. **Disorganized Attachment** - Known as *disoriented attachment*, this form occurs less commonly than other insecure attachments. It is sort of a mix of the other types, joining together the avoidant and anxious forms.

   It is an unpredictable form of connection that is reminiscent of chaos. This forms when the child has been a victim of abuse or trauma. They tend to move back and forth between pushing people away and a constant need for intimacy. Fear and neediness exist together in this form.

Past Trauma and Karma: Karma is a direct result of past trauma. When a person is faced with great difficulties, the unconscious develops a pattern of movements and actions to try to protect the individual from future failings and pain. As a result, karma is born, which is the reaction created to unresolved energy, causing the empath to play out specific actions as if they're acting out a prewritten script.

Karma is a direct result of past trauma.[27]

The higher self attempts to clear karma throughout one's journey and break the attachment to the trauma. This usually involves being placed in a similar position to the initial trauma to allow an opportunity to recognize the pattern and sever the attachment.

With some people, they may find themselves falling back on the same reaction their subconscious created to deal with the trauma. Therefore, the lesson is often repeated with higher energetic intensity every time until it is learned and the karma is cleared.

Clearing karma often involves two steps. The first is recognizing that you are stuck in karma, and the second is releasing said attachment.

Employing mindfulness allows the empath to monitor themselves as they start to enact the movements of karma. There are a number of methods used to release karma, such as forgiving yourself and others.

An upside of releasing karma is that a person doesn't only release themselves but also the person involved in creating it because, at its core, it is still an energy-based relationship. This is not naturally occurring. As you heal your own karma, you facilitate others' choice to heal themselves, as well.

Energetic Cords: As mentioned previously, cords of attachment can either be formed through love or fear, but they do not form unless permission has been granted consciously or subconsciously. Through daily interactions with people, an empath forms a separate cord with each person, varying in size depending on the depth of the relationship.

It is always a good idea to periodically check and evaluate the health of the cords connected to others. If there is a feeling of depletion from another person, it is sometimes best to cut the cord. With close family and friends, it is a good idea to practice clearing the cords connecting them. While these cords can be useful, they can sometimes turn into codependent cords. These types drain both people at both ends.

In a toxic relationship, the cord connecting an empath to the other person keeps them trapped in an old pattern, suffering negative emotions and preventing them from moving on. The same thing happens with cords formed with energy vampires, whether they are aware of the harm they're causing or not.

Being able to deal with this kind of mental and emotional invasion requires a lot of compassion and patience. Some of the practices used to break free of these cords include prayer, energetic exercises, acupuncture, and cord-cutting ceremonies.

Methods to Restore Vitality After an Energy Drain

Following an energy drain, especially one that may have taken a long time to recover from, it's important to engage in practices that restore one's center and allow you to take care of your well-being.

There are a few simple things you can do to recharge your batteries, so to speak, and return your energy flows to a stable position.

Journaling

Writing down emotions on paper is very revealing when looked back on. Not only does it serve as an outlet for negative and frustrating feelings, but it can also help gauge how the healing is progressing.

The act of pouring out your mind without focusing 100% on what's being written has a very cleansing effect on the energy and mind. It helps restore balance since it promotes a feeling of lightness after unloading the weight being carried around in the soul.

Energy can be visible in the written word, whether in the vocabulary being used or the handwriting itself. Noticing the subtle changes in the method of writing can help in readjusting the healing journey accordingly.

Yoga, Mindfulness, and Coloring Books

These practices are some of the most favored among healers to navigate energy drains. Whether you opt for a physical or mental option or both, these exercises help empaths stay grounded and reconnect them with the abundance of earth's energy.

Coloring is a simple yet effective way to take your mind off frustrating thoughts.*

Using coloring books or doing other simple activities, such as cleaning, can help take your mind off frustrating thoughts. Instead of overthinking, you'll find yourself focusing on the small tasks you need to finish and the lines you need to fill. Not to mention the rewarding sense of accomplishment felt in the end.

Take a Hot Shower or a Long Bath

It is common knowledge that washing and showering are among the most calming practices to use to reset yourself. Take your time and allow the water to drain away all the negative sensations you are experiencing.

People often mix it up with some visualization by imagining the water washing away fears and strains and replacing the energy with a cleaner kind.

Resting

Give yourself permission to rest if you need it. Sometimes, one of the hardest things is allowing yourself to listen to what your body tells you and take a day off or go to bed early. Having a good night's sleep allows you to wake up the next day with a refreshed sense of self, ready to deal with whatever is being thrown your way.

There are many other ways to restore energy after feeling drained, such as going on daily long walks or being around nature and animals. The most important aspect is to remember that you deserve to take care of yourself. You deserve protection and to take time for yourself to restore the part of your energy that has been tainted or depleted. Most importantly, you do not need to ask for permission to do so. The only permission you require is your own.

Protection After Cleansing

Following the energy work to restore the flow to a healthy state, it is vital to protect the achieved progress and improved state from any future invasions and intruding energies.

Set Boundaries and Create Distance: Empaths tend to absorb their surroundings, mimicking the characteristics of a sponge. It is important to use intuition to steer clear of any environments or people that trigger negative sensations.

Start by setting firm boundaries and holding them if the people causing you harm are not ones you can easily dispense of, like family members. Learn how to say no and stand your ground.

The second you sense your energy is being pulled in all other directions, start retreating. Don't wait until you're completely out. Look for another space where you can recharge and repair the damage endured.

Energetic Boundaries: There are several methods you can use when exploring energetic boundaries. You can use mindful visualizations to create a coat of armor around yourself and continuously drain out any negative energy into the universe and receive replenished new healthy flows.

You can utilize something more physical, like healing crystals. Crystals are used to create protective energy shields. Many empaths carry them around in their pockets everywhere they go to ensure constant protection.

Crystals, like black tourmaline, are among the strongest, well-known tools used by empaths to keep themselves grounded and safe. The way it works is that it absorbs negative energy, converting it into positive flows, which creates a shield from harmful influences.

Other examples include clear quartz, shungite, and selenite, which are often used to cleanse, strengthen, and protect their users.

Seek Support: When dealing with energy vampires and toxic environments, professional help comes in handy. Seek out the help of therapists or gurus to help you create shields around your energy that can limit any intruding negativity.

EXERCISE #1: Cutting Energy Cords

This ritual includes several steps that aim at cutting the emotional connection between you and the other party or event. These steps can start with exercising mindfulness through grounding, imagining the cord, severing the connection with both your mind and body, and then cleansing your aura or energy field afterward.

Instructions:

1. You can start the ritual with cleansing practices, such as having a salt bath to cleanse your energy flow.
2. Follow that with a smudging ritual. The smoke produced helps purify your energetic body and reconnect you with your higher self.
3. Write down your thoughts. Everything you've been meaning to tell the person or anything about the event affecting you. Pour it all down on paper. Once you're done, you can burn the paper as a sign of you releasing the negative influence and hold it had on you.
4. Start picturing the person you want to sever the cord with. Imagine yourself holding scissors in your hands. Reach out and connect to your higher self. Visualize the cord tethering you to the other person. With all the purpose you can muster, see yourself reaching with the scissors and cutting the cord. Watch as the two cord halves fall and retreat back within both of you. Remain still for a minute, feel your energy recover, and mentally thank the other person for the part they played in your story.
5. After the cord-cutting, some people prefer to use affirmations and say blessings. As an example, you can say, " I now cut all the cords that don't serve my well-being. All the energetic cords have been

severed across all times and planes. I take back my energy flows, replenishing me with health, vitality, peace and love."
6. After you're done, try to remain in a state of calm meditation. Sense your energy recharging back and take time to re-assimilate with it.
7. After you're done, picture yourself coated in a cloak of protective energy. This cloak of light and energy is the boundary that protects and helps you keep your energy levels high. Visualize the cloak in a steady form, remaining in place as you move on through your day.

EXERCISE #2: Energy Reset with Breathwork

There are several breathing exercises you can use to reset and recenter your energy. Among these is the Wim Hof breathing method.

Instructions:
1. This practice is best tried on an empty stomach, preferably as you wake up in the morning.
2. You can do the exercise sitting or lying down, as long as you're comfortable and your stomach has enough space to breathe.
3. Gently close your eyes and take a deep breath. Allow the breath to completely fill your lungs, and then slowly let it out without exerting effort in the exhale. Repeat 30 times.
4. After the 30th breath, hold your breath for as long as you can until you feel the urge to breathe again. You'll be surprised how long you're able to do that.
5. Take in another deep breath, hold for a count of 15 seconds, and then let it out.
6. Return back to the first step and repeat the process three times.

EXERCISE #3: Detachment Meditation

Detachment meditation operates in several stages.

Instructions:
1. Start with a comfortable position, whether lying down or sitting. Take a few deep breaths, and close your eyes.
2. Spend one minute examining the tension in your body. Where is it centered, where are you feeling it, and start releasing it?

3. Be intentional with your purpose, and repeat the mantra " I am letting go." The mantra can help you sharpen your mind. Spend one minute focusing on your intention.
4. Spend around 5 to 10 minutes focusing on your breath and the rhythm with which it's moving.
5. While breathing mindfully, you need to identify the attachments you're trying to break free from. Is it specific thoughts and beliefs, is it a toxic relationship, a harmful environment, or a traumatic event? Be honest with yourself. Observe these attachments as if they're floating around you.
6. Accept you don't always have control. You can't control others and natural events like the weather. You can't control the past, and you definitely can't control your whole community. Let go of what should've been and focus on what you can be. Accept what is and that life isn't always going to be fair.
7. Be self-aware. Examine your feelings towards these attachments and acknowledge them.
8. For 5 to 10 minutes, move your attention outside of your body. View your physical self as something separate from you.
9. Spend 10 more minutes letting go. Surrender yourself completely to the universe. Allow it to flow within you without fighting back. Place your mind at rest.
10. Finally, open your eyes and tell yourself you're surrendering yourself to the universe.

Chapter 7: SPIRITUAL HEALING I: Energy Healing Techniques for Empaths

Empaths have a higher need for regular energy healing and cleansing exercises. Their constant interactions with others' energies can leave them exhausted and out of balance. This chapter explores several healing techniques that can help you maintain your well-being.

Energy Healing for Empaths

Energy healing is a restorative approach designed to rebalance energetic states by balancing energy fields and clearing out blockages from the body, mind, and spirit. This holistic energy healing approach requires practitioners to use their hands to manipulate energy in the necessary direction. They may also use other instruments like acupuncture needles. Depending on the specific energy healing practice, practitioners may or may not touch the body of the person they are practicing on (it may be themselves, as experienced energy healers also know how to heal themselves).

Methods like reiki may be useful for manipulating energy.[39]

The basic principle of energy healing is that energy courses through and affects everything in the body, mind, and spirit, and any imbalance can cause issues in all these aspects of a person.

Restoring energetic balance will alleviate the symptoms and aid the healing process. Empaths are vulnerable to energetic imbalances, which cause them to have physical symptoms like pain and tension, emotional issues like a lack of control over their emotions, and other challenges that may hinder them from living a fulfilling life.

Empaths can absorb profuse amounts of negative energy, which leads to massive imbalances. Letting go can be challenging, so they may keep storing it until it completely overwhelms them. Energy healing can help empaths release the accumulated negative energy, clear out the energetic blockages it caused, and recharge with positivity. With practice, they can also learn to use energy healing to avoid depleting themselves of positive energy.

As with many other intuitive and spiritual practices, intent plays a crucial role in successful energy healing. To manipulate and channel energy to heal yourself or others, you must focus on your intention for restoring vitality. Before this, you must formulate a clear intention of what you want to accomplish. Then, you must clear your mind and body and concentrate on your intent. As you start the healing, keep your intention in your mind by reciting it several times. That will allow you to channel the energy in the way you want and that is most beneficial for you or the person you aim to heal.

Reiki for Empaths

Originating from ancient Japan and rediscovered during the 19th century by master Usui, Reiki is a hands-on healing practice based on energy channeling methods. Those who become attuned to Reiki energy can manipulate it, directing it with their hands into their body or someone else's for healing or rebalancing purposes.

While it takes time and practice to master Reiki, anyone can start the journey simply by following its basic principles:

- *Just for today, I will not be angry:* Promotes the practice of letting go of anger instead of letting it accumulate and fester, tainting a person's energy.

- *Just for today, I will not worry:* Likewise, letting go of worries about past experiences and what the future may bring is beneficial for restoring balance.

- *Just for today, I will be grateful:* Fosters gratitude toward what someone has instead of despairing over what they don't have.

- *Just for today, I will do my work honestly:* Giving your best at work will lead to a much more fulfilling existence.

- *Just for today, I will be kind to every living thing:* By following this principle, you learn to be compassionate toward others and, eventually, be kinder to yourself.

To adhere to these Reiki teachings, you can incorporate them into your daily life. For example, you can set the intention to let go of anger and worries, express gratitude for something, work honestly, and perform an act of kindness every day. It won't take much time before you start feeling the effects of your energy being rebalanced.

Are you wondering how Reiki would be beneficial for you as an empath? One of the major benefits of using Reiki energy for healing is that you won't get depleted in the process. The life force will flow through you and into the entity you want to heal, but it won't take your energy. In fact, it can ground the excess energy you may have picked up from others. It can help you tell whether the emotions you're experiencing are yours or someone else's. By grounding it, you'll be able to identify your energy and clear out the rest. Reiki can even help you calm down when you get overwhelmed by the emotions you've absorbed.

Tip: Recite the Reiki principles when you want to soothe and center yourself.

Should you find that the energy you absorb from others blocks your energy centers or causes them to fall out of balance, Reiki can help remedy this, too. It counters negativity, especially if you use it to create an automatic shield for yourself before you start interacting with others. If you still absorb some negativity after shielding up, you can connect to the Reiki energy and use it to cleanse yourself, clear energetic blockages, and restore emotional balance within yourself.

Self-Reiki for Emotional Healing

Here is your first exercise to start self-healing with Reiki.

Instructions:

1. Find a quiet space where you won't be disturbed and sit comfortably.
2. Take a few deep breaths to relax your body and mind, then bring an emotional issue you want to heal into focus.
3. Now, place your hand on your heart chakra, which is located in the middle of your chest, behind your sternum.
4. Set the intention of directing the universal energy toward your heart chakra.
5. Focusing on your breath, inhale deeply. While you do, visualize a white light appearing around your hand.
6. The light starts to travel from your hand and into your body. This is the healing energy permeating through you. Visualize your body lighting up part by part until the energy clears any blockages.

The Fingers Method

If you find it challenging to channel the universal energy with your hands, it may be easier to use just your fingers.

Instructions:

1. Find a quiet space, get comfortable, and relax by taking deep breaths.
2. Raise your hands in front of you, palms down, and spread your fingers open. Then, bunch up your fingers together, stretching them as if trying to grab a small item.

3. Spread them open again, then bunch them up again, and continue alternating between the two poses for a few minutes. This helps connect with universal energy because people use their fingers to touch everything, and their fingers can be a vessel for the energy.
4. As you continue stretching and gathering your fingers, see the energy materialize around them. See it enter your fingers, allowing it to manipulate it as you wish. For example, after stretching, you can spread the energy around your body to create a shield to repel negative energy and emotions.

The Windmill Channeling

This is another method for channeling healing energy toward yourself.

Instructions:
1. Find a quiet space, get comfortable, and relax.
2. Raise your hands to your sides at shoulder level. Make a tight fist with both.
3. Rotate your wrists, making a small circle with them. Don't move your elbow and shoulder while rotating your wrists.
4. Repeat the previous step at least five times for both wrists. In the second repetition, visualize energy moving around your wrists while roasting them. See it go up and down just as your knuckles do. Round and round in a circle, becoming concentrated around your hands.
5. As you continue your repetitions, set the intention of channeling the energy toward yourself. As you move your wrists around, the energy starts flowing into your body, empowering and rebalancing it.

Qi Gong for Empaths

According to Traditional Chinese Medicine (TCM) principles, the vital energy coursing through all bodies, the qi, is responsible for keeping the body healthy and balanced. Qi can fall out of balance, and when it does, it's necessary to cultivate and rebalance it. One of the popular methods TCM uses to establish balance within the body is Qi Gong.

Born out of the conjunction of the words "qi" (meaning vital energy) and "gong" (meaning a skill acquired by training), Qi Gong is a name of a unique practice. It relies on intention setting, movement, and breathwork to heal and rebalance a person's energetic landscape. When a person starts experiencing difficulties in their body, it's likely because their energy is blocked or can't flow freely through their body. This is where Qi Gong comes in handy. It channels qi and removes obstacles from its way so it can flow freely. Empaths can absorb and accumulate lots of stagnant and negative energy, which can hinder the flow of positive energy in their body. Through regular Qi Gong practice, they can move the bad energy out of the way, thus clearing energy blockages, getting stagnant energy moving, and letting positive energy move freely.

Qi Gong for Energy Flow

Here is a basic Qi Gong exercise to improve energy flow within your body.

Instructions:
1. Find a quiet space where you won't be disturbed. Get comfortable and start taking deep breaths.
2. As you relax, set your intention to get your energy moving.
3. Continue breathing deeply while raising your arms above your head, palms up. Imagine you're pushing the energy toward the sky. Visualize the energy moving through your body with each breath you take.
4. Lower your hands, then raise them back again. While your hands are lowered, imagine you're drawing more energy from the ground. You're gathering the energy and pushing it toward the sky, letting it travel through you, empowering you, healing you, and allowing you to become a better empath.
5. Continue the "pushing the sky" and the "gathering energy" movements until you feel your body replenished with vital life force and all stagnant energy has left your body.

Opening and Closing Posture for Breathing Awareness

By bringing closer awareness to your breathing, your Qi Gong exercises will become more effective, and you'll even be able to benefit from more focused breathing while healing yourself or others as an empath.

Instructions:
1. Stand with your feet slightly wider than shoulder-width apart. Bend your knees slightly and raise your hands in front of you, opening them to shoulder-width.

2. Take a deep breath, and as you prepare to release it, start pushing your hands towards each other. As the air leaves your lungs, your hands get closer and closer to each other. Don't let them touch.
3. Continue breathing in and out through your nose, with your tongue placed gently on your upper palate.
4. Open your hands to shoulder width again. Repeat several more times. Starting from the following repetition, visualize a magnetic force between your hands. See it pulling hands together as you breathe in, and do your best to withstand the pull as you breathe out.
5. Visualize the qi circulating downwards as you exhale and upwards as you inhale. Use your intuition to show you where the qi will travel. For example, it can go in a straight line, form an orb, become diffused into tiny particles, etc.

Healing Touch Therapy

As another hands-on method for emotional, physical, and spiritual recovery, healing touch therapy also uses energy as its tool for creating balance and starting the rejuvenating process. Practitioners may touch the body of the person they're trying to heal or skim the air or another surface near the body. They use the healing touch to eliminate blockages and hindrances in a person's energetic landscape, restoring the health and vitality of those who are being treated.

Before the sessions, practitioners of healing touch therapy must ground themselves, entering into a higher state of consciousness. They assess the energy field of the person seeking healing or rebalancing by moving their hands over or slightly above their body. They look for imbalances or signs that these may be present. Then, they opt for one of the healing touch techniques they can use to eliminate imbalances. For example, they can move their hands across the body, stopping at each chakra (energy center), with special attention to those that appear blocked or out of balance. Or, they move their hands across the other person's energy field without touching them. This is a good option if the person is already experiencing physical symptoms, so the practitioner knows what area of the body they should focus on. They start scanning the energy field right there and identify and clear blockages very effectively. Lastly, the practitioners help the other person ground themselves with their renewed energy, which will prevent them from absorbing negative energy.

Healing touch therapy can help relieve pain and anxiety – two symptoms that often plague empaths who absorb and retain too much negative energy from others. Healing touch therapy can help them remove the negative energy from the body, effectively mending them and alleviating their symptoms.

Sound Healing (Binaural Beats and Tibetan Bowls)

Sounds carry vibrations that have an immense effect on a person's body, mind, and spirit. One of these is slowing down brain waves. When the brain reduces its activity in a calm state, it creates alpha or theta waves. During these, a person is in a dreamlike state without being asleep. However, the person can relax and relieve their anxiety and symptoms of physical health conditions, just like when they're working on restoring themselves during sleep.

Sound healing uses various methods to induce relaxing brain waves and help a person heal and soothe themselves. Usually, the practice requires you to get comfortable and listen to certain sounds like binaural beats, gongs, chimes, or Tibetan singing bowls. While you relax to these sounds, the energy and vibrations of the sounds travel across your body, restoring its energetic balance. The vibrations connect with your energy, effectively filling you with positive and uplifting energy that can counter the negative energy you absorb from others as an empath.

Crystal Healing

Crystals have their own unique energies and vibrations and can absorb energies you want to charge them with. For the same reason, empaths can use crystals to absorb negative energy, heal, or clear energy blockages in themselves or others.

There are plenty of crystals that can be used for healing and energy balancing, with the most effective ones being:

- **Clear Quartz:** Besides cleansing and healing, this crystal can amplify the positive energy you charge them with. It can also improve focus so you can channel your healing intention more effectively.

Clear Quartz.[30]

- **Amethyst:** It fosters a deeper connection with your intuition. It can also be useful during the cleansing phase of any spiritual practice and offers protection against unwanted energies.

Amethyst.[31]

- **Rose Quartz:** A powerful emotional healer, this crystal is known for its gentle color but all the more potent ability to attract loving energy. You can use it to achieve faster self-love and kindness while healing from the negative energies you absorb.

Rose Quartz.[32]

- **Citrine:** Warm as the sun, this crystal can help attract light and positive energy, balance your emotional landscape, and contribute to the success of your healing practice. It stimulates chakras, making them absorb more positive energy.

Citrine.[33]

- **Carnelian:** If you feel unmotivated to continue interacting with others' energies, this crystal can give you the boost you need to keep going. It can show you how strong and resilient you can be through healing and restoring your balance.

Carnelian.[84]

- **Black Tourmaline:** Another powerful protective crystal often used for calming and grounding. It has a direct link to the Earth's energy, and you can use it to channel negative energy into it and exchange it for positive energy through the ground.

Black Tourmaline.[85]

- **Selenite:** This crystal is best used to cleanse your other crystals but can also bring you clarity during your healing and restorative sessions. Its vibrations are incredibly pure. Some even use them to reach spiritual enlightenment.

Selenite.[86]

- **Lapis Lazuli:** This crystal is an excellent choice for those seeking additional wisdom or awareness of the path ahead. It can help you find new insights and strengthen your connection with your intuition and inner self. All this can be beneficial throughout the healing process.

Lapis Lazuli.[87]

- **Red Jasper:** Another stone for grounding and stability. It's especially handy when you feel anxious, which may hinder you in your healing endeavors, or when you want to alleviate symptoms of anxiety in others. It fosters tranquility, empowering the healing and rebalancing process.

Red Jasper.[88]

Additional Recommendations

Acupressure

Acupressure is another practice rooted in TCM. It entails using pressure on specific points of the body to alleviate pain, tension, and stress. Acupuncture, a similar practice, works on the same principle, except it involves placing thin needles along the same points. According to TCM, pressure or puncture is applied along the pathway of energy coursing through the body. Like chakras in other practices and belief systems, these pressure points can be used to access and rebalance energy within the body.

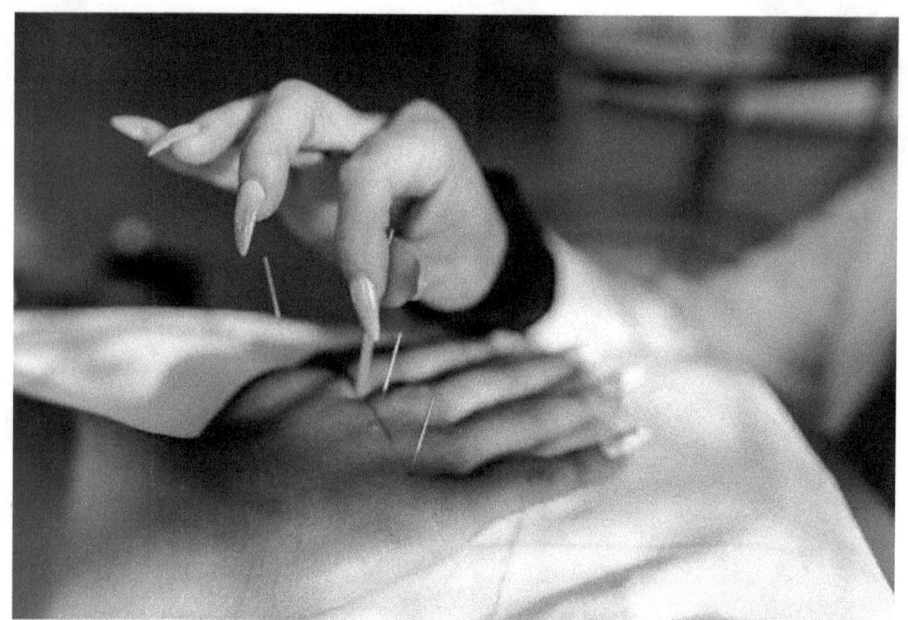
Acupuncture, like acupressure, focuses on specific pressure points for healing.[89]

One of the main advantages of acupressure is that you can perform some of its techniques by yourself. As an empath, you may benefit from applying pressure on your acupoints, as it may help restore the energetic balance you lost after absorbing negative energies from others. It may also help restore the qi (vital energy) when you feel drained and exhausted. Stimulating these points can also alleviate physical symptoms of carrying around excess energy.

Some acupoints you can use to alleviate your symptoms and restore your energetic balance include the spot between your eyebrows, the top of your head, and the spot where your shoulders and neck meet. You can massage these with a circular motion, applying light pressure. You can also apply a gentle pinching move between your thumb and your index finger or between your big toe and your second toe. Once you pinch these spots, hold for several moments until you feel relief.

Bioresonance Therapy

Bioresonance therapy operates on a similar principle to sound healing. Instead of vibrations, this method focuses on detecting and interacting with electromagnetic waves emitted by the body. According to practitioners, these waves emanate from every cell of the body and can give clues about the person's well-being.

By analyzing the electromagnetic waves, it's possible to detect energetic imbalances within the body and counter these to restore balance in the energetic landscape. It aids the body's natural healing processes, which is why it's highly recommended for empaths. Empaths have their own healing mechanisms disrupted by the negative energies and emotions they absorb.

By considering the empath's energetic makeup after accumulating others' energies, bioresonance therapy can help address their imbalances effectively. Another massive benefit is that bioresonance therapy can address not only physical but also mental and emotional symptoms. It relies on a holistic approach that dictates that all aspects of a person's well-being can affect and cause disturbances in the person's energetic system, and these can be detected through electromagnetic waves. In other words, it addresses the root causes of a person's health issues, which, for empaths, is most likely the negative energy they absorb and accumulate while interacting with others.

EFT

Also known as tapping, EFT is another method relying on the principles of TCM. Like acupressure or acupuncture, EFT also accesses the body's energy through the meridian pathways and the specific points on which it accumulates.

EFT can also alleviate physical, mental, and emotional symptoms of energetic imbalances by restoring harmony and allowing the person's energy to flow freely and without disruptions.

Empaths may benefit from EFT tapping as it can help them restore balance in their energy system and relieve stress, anxiety, and tension caused by stagnant energy they pick up. With a few targeted taps of the fingertips, EFT can work wonders for restoring your well-being. EFT works best if the main symptom has been identified because this allows the practitioner to focus on one problem at a time.

Tapping can be applied in a range of intensities, and practitioners usually test for the intensity that works best for each person. Then, they tap in a sequence across nine points of the person's energetic pathway. These include the top of the head, the side of the eye, the eyebrow, under the eye, the side of the hand, under the nose, the chin, the beginning of the collarbone, and under the arm.

While applying the tapping sequences, the person who needs healing is encouraged to acknowledge any issue they may have. This is an empowering approach that further aids the effect of the tapping. For example, if you, as an empath, can embrace your abilities despite knowing how much stress picking up on others' emotions and energies can cause you, this will tremendously boost your healing process.

Aromatherapy

Aromatherapy uses the brain's ability to soothe itself after registering a calming trigger through one of the senses. The aromatic stimuli applied in aromatherapy reach the olfactory senses located in the nose. What brings the stimuli there? Aromatherapy uses essential oils, which are broken down into tiny molecules. These molecules are released into the air and reach the person's nose. There, they are picked up and cause a chain reaction that results in the brain releasing hormones that affect the person's emotional landscape. The oils influencing the nervous system prompt the person to take control over their emotions and calm themselves.

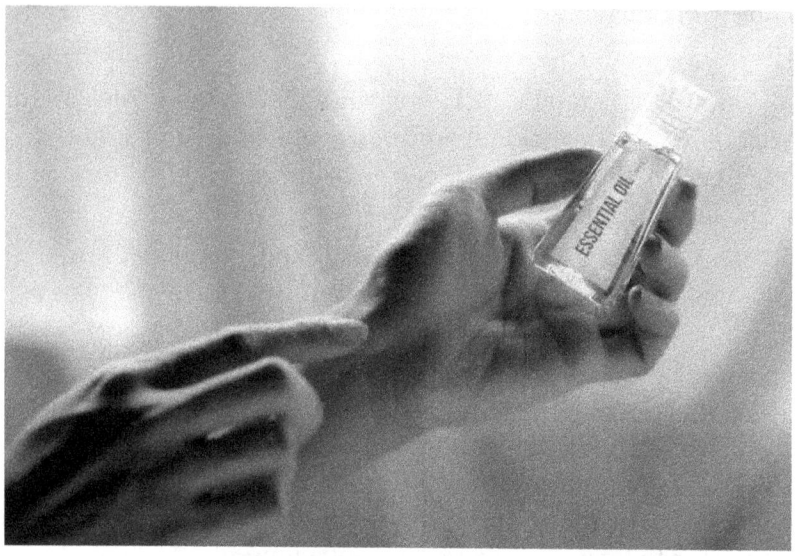

Aromatherapy triggers certain parts of the brain to instigate healing.[40]

For empaths, aromatherapy can be an effortless yet incredibly powerful tool for emotional healing. It can help reduce the anxiety you feel after getting worked up on someone else's behalf when you pick up on the stress they are experiencing. It can also boost your mood and alleviate symptoms of depression caused by all the negative emotions and energy you absorb from others over time. Aromatherapy may also relieve physical symptoms like pain and tension caused by energetic disturbances and blockages.

Some of the most recommended essential oils for empaths are lavender, chamomile, sage, geranium, bergamot, jasmine, frankincense, laurel, mandarin, lemon, pine, patchouli, rose, sweet orange, sandalwood, and ylang-ylang.

Massage Therapy

Massage therapy can also help release negative energy in the form of tension and pain. Empaths who pick up copious amounts of anxiety, sadness, and other negative emotions (which then become trapped in their body) can benefit from various massage modalities aimed at promoting relaxation and releasing the trapped emotions. They foster better emotional balance by targeting pressure points where the energy becomes trapped and causes blockages. Massage therapy can also prompt the brain to release beneficial hormones that soothe the nervous system, causing a person to feel better. This subjective sensation of well-being further enhances the effect of energy release and rebalancing achieved through massage therapy.

Several massage modalities can help empaths reach a better emotional and energetic state. These include deep tissue massage, myofascial release, trigger point therapy, petrissage, and effleurage, as well as massage combined with breathwork.

Deep Tissue Massage

Unlike tapping or acupressure, deep tissue massage involves using a much firmer and prolonged form of pressure. By spreading the pressure across larger portions of the body, the tension-releasing effect becomes much stronger. Empaths who have accumulated negative emotions and stress over a longer period may benefit from this healing massage technique. It can release large amounts of trapped emotions after only one or a few applications.

Trigger Point Therapy

Sometimes, tension due to emotional overload can accumulate in body parts other than muscles. However, the accumulation still begins in the major muscle groups (most empaths can attest to feeling tense in the major muscle groups from time to time), but then the stress is transmitted to other body parts. The areas that project the pain and stress are called trigger points. By massaging them, they can be prevented from transmitting trapped emotions and releasing them instead. Trigger point therapy entails applying pressure to the projection points, promoting emotional release.

Myofascial Discharge

This massage modality targets the fascia, effectively discharging stress from it. The fascia is the protective tissue enveloping the body's organs and muscles. It stores more stagnant energy and emotions than any other part of the physical body, and manipulating it can help move them. Besides releasing pain and tension, this massage can also restore emotional vitality to empaths struggling with the overload of stagnant emotions.

Massage Combined with Breathwork

These techniques usually integrate deep breathing exercises into the massage sessions. This enriches the relaxing effect of the massage, allowing for a much deeper release. A person can start the deep breathing exercise before receiving massage therapy, using it to release tension from the massage points or integrate it afterward to completely let go of the recently released emotions. For empaths, integrating breathwork into massage is a wonderful way to focus their intention to heal and release their (and everyone else's) emotions. It can contribute to their physical, mental, and emotional health and well-being tremendously.

Petrissage and Effleurage

Petrissage (kneading movements) and effleurage (gliding movements) are two unique massage modalities that involve using gentle stroking moves to reduce anxiety in the mind and tension in the body's soft tissues. Empaths may benefit from them as they evoke profound, calming, and relaxing sensations throughout the body. Petrissage and effleurage also foster a sense of safety that allows you to let go of all the emotional burdens you've absorbed and accumulated.

Chapter 8: SPIRITUAL HEALING II: Unblock and Enhance Your Empathic Abilities

You shouldn't just focus on healing your energy and protecting yourself from negative people and emotions. You also need to enhance your gift and grow as an empath. This chapter helps you navigate your empathic abilities to overcome your emotional blocks. It provides you with the necessary tools to boost your confidence and resilience and help you embrace your unique empathic abilities.

Your empathy is a gift.⁴¹

Connecting with Your Empathic Gifts

Your empathic abilities are in your nature.

Your empathy is a part of you that you shouldn't try to get rid of or fight. You should embrace it and see it as a strength instead of a burden. Understandably, this isn't always easy. When you constantly feel drained and socialization becomes taxing, empathy can feel more like a curse than a blessing.

However, empathy is a gift you should nourish and embrace as part of your soul's blueprint and mission in life. Many people wish they could connect with others, relate to their experiences, and feel their pain like you do. Sometimes, a spouse sees their partner upset but doesn't know how to connect with them. A person who has never had a bad breakup may struggle to relate to their friend who is going through a divorce.

These individuals probably feel helpless for failing to help their loved ones and understand their pain. Who doesn't want to be more empathetic and attuned to other people's emotions? You have a gift that many wish for, so you should appreciate your unique abilities.

You can connect and embrace your empathy with these tips.

Understand Your Unique Nature

Empaths should learn about themselves, understand their unique abilities, and explore their sensitivity. This will help you see that your empathy is in your nature and a gift, not a curse. Empathy isn't a personality trait you can outgrow; it is a part of who you are that you should accept, not fight.

Distinguish Between Your Feelings and Other People's Emotions

Empaths constantly absorb other people's emotions and can't always tell whether these feelings are theirs or someone else's. You need to be attuned to your physical sensations to recognize any sudden shift in your energy. Whenever you feel sad, angry, frustrated, etc., ask yourself, "Are these feelings mine?" Mindful exercises such as meditation and breathwork can make you present and aware of your internal experience so you can notice when something external affects your mood.

Accept Your Vulnerabilities

Allow yourself to be vulnerable to fully understand people's different emotions. Many people have been raised to believe that vulnerability is a sign of weakness. You need to change these thoughts and embrace this part of yourself. Express your feelings to your loved ones, open up to them, and don't be afraid to show your fears and weaknesses.

Blocks to Empathy – 1. Overcoming Doubt and Fear

Many empaths see their gift as a curse and often experience self-doubt or fear their abilities. You may believe that navigating your empathy can be challenging and hold you back in life. However, these are limiting beliefs that distort your reality and prevent you from achieving your goals and living your life. You need to change this mindset to overcome your doubts and fears.

Your Sensitivity Isn't a Weakness

Oftentimes, people struggle with embracing their empathic abilities because they believe that their sensitivity is a weakness. However, your empathy and sensitivity are sources of strength. They allow you to understand others, connect with them on a deeper level, and build trust and rapport with them.

You need to challenge this negative belief.

- Ask yourself what proof you have that sensitivity makes you weak. Reflect on all the times you or someone you know was sensitive towards another person's feelings, and you will realize it requires confidence, resilience, and strength.
- Why do you associate empathy with weakness? Some people think that if they are viewed as sensitive, they will lose respect or won't be able to control the situation (this is specifically true if you are in a leadership position). However, imagine how people will respond to you when you show kindness, compassion, and sensitivity.

Reflect on Past Moments

Reflect on past moments when your empathy helped you connect with others or solve a problem. Write these moments in your journal and read them each time you experience doubts and fears about your abilities.

Reframe Your Thoughts

Reframe your beliefs with positive thoughts to change your mindset and make yourself feel empowered. For instance, instead of saying, "My sensitivity is a source of weakness," say, "My sensitivity is my biggest strength and empowers me every day."

Blocks to Empathy – 2. Past Wounds and Trapped Emotions

Past emotional wounds can block the natural flow of your empathic energy. According to a 2023 study conducted by Chongqing Normal University in China and the Department of Education Sciences and Professional Programs, University of Missouri, people who experienced emotional neglect in their childhood lack empathy in their adulthood.

Suppose your parents didn't meet your emotional needs. In that case, you won't be able to understand, sympathize, or respond to other people's pain. For instance, you come home crying because your best friend is moving to another state, and you won't see them again. Instead of hugging and comforting you, your parents dismissed your feelings, belittled them, or ignored you.

Parents are a child's first role models. They are supposed to teach you how to love, express your feelings, and deal with your emotions. However, if they aren't emotionally supportive, you will never learn how to handle strong emotions or act when someone is sad, crying, or expressing their feelings to you. As a result, you may appear cold and distant.

Healing these emotional blocks can improve your empathic abilities, release your trapped emotions, and help you move on from your past wounds. Try these gentle techniques to help with your emotional healing.

Inner-Child Work

Say when you were nine or ten years old, one of your classmates made fun of you, and your whole class laughed at you. You went home crying, hoping your parents would comfort you, but they yelled at you for expressing your emotions or were too busy to notice you, leaving you feeling alone and neglected.

While this memory may have faded, you can't forget being mocked, crying, and your parents' neglect. When you were a child, you promised yourself never to show vulnerability again or let anyone see your cry, and you kept that promise to this day.

You haven't moved on from your past wounds, and your inner child is still in control of your emotional reactions. Inner-child work is recognizing and healing your childhood emotional trauma. It's understanding that your current reactions stem from your painful past.

Inner-child work reconnects you with your wounded self and gives it the love, attention, and other needs you were deprived of in your childhood. This helps you be more resilient and gives your adult self-control over your emotional reactions.

- **Listen to Your Inner Child:** Pay attention to your triggers. Do specific people cause you emotional pain? Do some places or situations make you angry or upset? Write down in your journal any sudden changes in your mood or behavior and what caused them to understand your triggers.
- **Meditate:** Meditation increases your self-awareness, allowing you to recognize any changes in your emotional state. It also reduces your stress and helps you develop emotional regulation skills.
- **Be Your Own Parent:** Your parents may have done the best they could, but nobody's perfect. Children don't come with an instruction book. All parents make mistakes, even the most well-intentioned ones. Others can be toxic, leaving you to deal with many emotional issues. Either way, you may not have had your emotional needs met as a child. Instead of holding grudges or getting stuck in the past, give yourself the love, compassion, and emotional support no one gave you in your childhood. Practice self-care, cheer yourself on, and support yourself. When your inner child is upset, step up and be the parent you never had.
- **Speak to Your Parents:** Children see their parents as the only two adults who have all the answers and don't make any mistakes. However, your parents are human beings with weaknesses, flaws, and their own traumas. Speak to them to understand why they weren't emotionally supportive. You may find they had a traumatic childhood or their own parents didn't meet their emotional needs. As a result, they didn't have role models to teach them how to be good parents. While there is no excuse for abusing one's child, learning about your parents' past experiences can give you closure. You may find they didn't know any better. You may even sympathize with their past, leading you to repair your relationship with them and heal your inner child.

Forgiveness

You can't go back and change the past or keep holding grudges that will only cause you more pain. You need to forgive your parents, caretakers, ex-partner, or those who caused your emotional wounds. Forgiveness doesn't mean you should forget what happened to you. Sometimes, you can't erase the painful memories from your mind, and that's okay.

Some people struggle with this step. They believe that if someone hasn't apologized or shown remorse, they don't deserve to be forgiven. However, forgiveness has nothing to do with the other person. Your anger only hurts you and ruins your present and future. It keeps you connected to your traumatic past and the toxic person.

Forgiveness sets you free, allows you to put the past behind you, and pushes you to move on with your life. Don't waste your years waiting for an apology that will never come. No one will give you closure but you.

According to Shanita Brown, a licensed clinical mental health counselor and teaching assistant professor at East Carolina University, parents don't know how to apologize. Dr. Brown suggests that you should learn about your parents' lives. When you stop seeing your mother and father as superheroes, you will find it easier to forgive them. If you are uncomfortable talking to them, you can ask your aunts or uncles about your parents' lives before you were born. This will help you sympathize with them and be more compassionate and understanding of their experience.

You can practice the same tactic with a toxic ex-partner or the person who caused your trauma. Ask a mutual friend or someone from their family about their past and upbringing. This will help humanize them, making it easier to forgive them.

Write a letter to your parents or abusive partner expressing your feelings, explaining all the pain they caused you, and telling them that you forgive them. However, don't send the letter. You can keep it or burn it as a way to symbolize letting go of the past.

Cutting Energetic Cords

Some cultures believe you form an energetic chord with your loved ones, which connects you to them. In toxic relationships, these cords can impact your inner peace and personal growth. You need to cut the cord and release the negative emotional ties.

Instructions:
1. Set intentions to cleanse your space and release negative energy. Light sage and use the smoke to cleanse the room.
2. Bring a string and place it before you.
3. Imagine that this string is the energetic chord connecting you to a toxic person from your past.

4. Cut the string with scissors to sever the ties with the past.
5. Throw the string in the trash.

Blocks to Empathy – 3. Mental Limitations

You may believe you are too sensitive or that your empathic abilities aren't practical, which can subconsciously limit your abilities. You can overcome these beliefs and break through these mental limitations with affirmations.

Affirmations

- *I embrace my empathic abilities that help me understand others.*
- *My sensitivity is my greatest strength and allows me to have genuine connections with others.*
- *I can protect myself from negative energy and toxic people.*
- *I am attuned to my emotions and can manage them wisely.*
- *I embrace my emotions as they are part of my empathic nature.*
- *My intuition guides me to healthy people and relationships.*
- *My empathic abilities will help me heal from emotional pain.*
- *I protect my energy and emotions from energy vampires and manipulators.*
- *I am happy and at peace with my empathic abilities.*
- *I can help others without draining my energy.*
- *My sensitivity gives me strength.*
- *I cherish relationships that respect my empathic nature.*
- *I take time to recharge my energy and protect my mental health.*
- *I have the tools to face challenges with a calm mind.*
- *I have the power to heal and grow.*
- *I am proud of my empathic nature.*

Blocks to Empathy – 4. Physical Blockages

Your body can hold on to stress and emotional trauma, which can affect your empathic abilities. This part focuses on exercises that can cleanse and heal your body to release physical blockages.

Walking Consciously

Choose a place that gives you peace and walk through it consciously.⁴⁸

Instructions:

1. Choose a safe and quiet place with limited or no distractions, such as a park or your garden.
2. Wear comfortable shoes and clothes.
3. Stand still and pay attention to your physical sensations.
4. Take a few deep breaths and focus on the present moment.
5. Walk slower than normal, but be mindful of your surroundings and your internal and external experiences.
6. Feel how your heels, toes, leg muscles, and body move with each step.
7. Feel the wind in your hair, listen to the birds in the sky, feel the grass under your feet, and see the trees around you.
8. Notice each breath as you inhale and exhale.
9. Breathe slowly and deeply.
10. If your mind wanders, refocus on your breathing.
11. After you finish, stand still and take a few deep breaths.

Shaking (Qi Gong)

Instructions:
1. Find a quiet place with no distractions. It should be wide enough to allow you to move freely.
2. Stand with your feet shoulder-width apart with your knees slightly bent. Relax your shoulders and straighten your spine.
3. Take a few long, deep breaths to center yourself.
4. Breathe in through your nostrils and breathe out through your mouth.
5. Shake your heels to create a vibration that travels through your body.
6. Shake your torso, legs, and arms. You can shake your entire body or each body part at a time.
7. Dance, shake your hands, twist your torso, or add any other movement while taking deep, slow breaths.
8. While you shake, let go of any stress or tension in your body.
9. Practice for ten minutes.
10. After you finish, stand still and focus on how your body feels.

Yoga

Low Lunge Pose Instructions:

Low lunge pose.⁴⁸

1. Begin in the down dog position.
2. Take a few deep breaths.
3. Put your right foot forward and place it behind your right hand.
4. Your right knee should be over your ankle.
5. Lower your left knee to the ground.
6. Lift your hands and place them over your right thigh.
7. Press your feet into the ground, straighten your spine, and lift the top of your head.
8. Stretch your arms up high with your palms facing each other.
9. Stay in this position for a couple of minutes, then repeat on the other side.

Pranayama (Breathing Exercises)

Kapalabhati (Skull Shining Breath) Instructions:

1. Breathe normally through your nose.
2. Start exhaling forcibly through your nose in short, regular bursts.
3. Each time you exhale, bring your abdominal muscles to your spine to release the air from your body.
4. Breathe in naturally, but breathe out forcibly.
5. Keep your shoulders, neck, and head neutral. Only allow your abdomen to move each time you exhale.
6. Repeat 20 times.

Tips and Exercises to Enhance Your Empathic Intuition

Strengthening the Third Eye

Meditation Instructions:

1. Find a quiet place with no distractions.
2. Sit comfortably and close your eyes.
3. Focus your mind's eye, your third eye. It's the space between your eyebrows.
4. Visualize a radiant light coming out of your third eye and flowing through your body.

5. Feel as it expands your inner awareness.
6. Focus on this image for a few minutes.
7. If unwanted thoughts interrupt your meditation, observe them without judgment and refocus on your visualization.

Working with Your Higher Self and Spirit Guides

Instructions:

1. Sit comfortably and take long, deep breaths until your mind and body start to relax.
2. Close your eyes and imagine yourself surrounded by white light. It surrounds your whole body, from your feet to the top of your head, keeping you safe.
3. Imagine you are on an island and see a path in front of you.
4. You walk along the path and see beautiful trees and hear the birds singing in the sky.
5. At the end of the path, you find a beautiful meadow. You sit on the grass and ask your higher self to join you.
6. You feel a change in the air. You look and find a golden light next to you.
7. You notice the light starts to take shape. It transforms into a beautiful being that takes your breath away.
8. Imagine their clothes, hair, looks, etc.
9. You feel comfortable and at peace around this being. It is your higher self.
10. You see a golden cord comes from this being and attaches to you. You are now connected.
11. Be still and notice if you receive messages from your higher self. You may see an image, symbol, or word or experience a physical sensation.
12. Ask your higher self any question you want and notice what you see, hear, or feel.
13. After you finish, thank your higher self for its wisdom, take a few deep breaths, open your eyes, and return to reality.
14. Write down everything you have experienced and try to find what your higher self was trying to communicate to you.

15. Repeat this technique each time you want to communicate with your higher self.
16. You can use this exercise to connect with your spirit guides. Just visualize the light transforming into your spirit guide and communicate with it.

Advanced Energy Protection and Shielding
Instructions:
1. Sit comfortably and close your eyes.
2. Take a few long, deep breaths.
3. Imagine a bubble made of white light surrounding you.
4. The bubble is alive and protecting you.
5. It is a shield protecting you from energy vampires and toxic people.
6. Imagine the bubble expanding, making you feel safe and calm.
7. If you need extra protection or feel vulnerable to other people's negative energy, pull the bubble closer and tighter to your body.
8. You have now created an energy field that will always protect you.

Mastering Energy Boundaries

- When you set boundaries, don't worry about how people will react. Toxic individuals will try to guilt-trip you or make you feel selfish for prioritizing your needs. Your boundaries are meant to protect you, so don't listen to anyone else but yourself.

- You set boundaries according to your values and what makes you comfortable. Don't let anyone interfere or dictate what you should or shouldn't tolerate.

- Say no to people or situations that drain your energy. If someone makes plans, but you want time to be alone or recharge, say no. Your loved ones will respect your boundaries, but toxic people will push their limits, so be careful.

- Don't be a people pleaser at the expense of your happiness and mental health. Take care of yourself and prioritize peace of mind.

Practicing Energy Transmutation

This involves transforming negative energy into high and uplifting vibration.

- Be aware of your thoughts and emotions to recognize when your energy changes.
- Positivity attracts positive thoughts and emotions. Focus on the things that bring you joy and put you in a good mood.
- Exercise every day to distract yourself from the negativity and focus on your body's movements. Physical activities release endorphins, which reduce stress and improve your mood.
- Journaling, breathing exercises, meditation, and other mindful techniques can teach you to focus on the present moment instead of thinking of the past or worrying about the future, which takes away from today's joy and peace of mind.

Raising Vibrations for Enhanced Sensitivity

- Smile.
- Laugh.
- Perform an act of kindness, like feeding stray cats and dogs or complimenting someone.
- Pray or practice spiritual activities like meditation.
- Write down three things you are grateful for every day.
- Practice visualization.
- Spend time in nature.
- Listen to music.

Refining Empathic Senses

- Work on your listening skills. Instead of listening to respond or give an opinion, make the other person feel heard and understood. Create a safe space for them to express their feelings without judgment, make eye contact, and ask open-ended questions to keep the conversation going.
- Put yourself in other people's shoes and be compassionate and supportive.

- Don't make assumptions about others, and examine your biases. Forming opinions based on someone's race, gender, or age will prevent you from understanding their personal experience and empathizing with them.
- Be curious about people and believe you can learn something from everyone you meet.

Channeling Empathic Gifts for Service to Others

Your empathy and sensitivity are gifts you should use to help others and make the world a better place. Use your abilities to make people feel seen and heard. Let them know you understand what they are going through and that you can feel their pain. Listen to them and provide a shoulder to cry on without judgment or waiting for something in return. Some people may struggle to express their feelings and needs, so use your unique abilities and support them before they say a word. Be kind and compassionate to everyone you meet. However, don't forget to take care of yourself and focus on your needs.

Final Encouragement and Tips for Building Daily Empathic Rituals

Never forget that your empathy is a part of you and makes you the great person you are. Use your unique abilities to help others and grow as a person. Your empathy doesn't have to be a burden. The tips in the book will help you deal with past wounds and protect yourself from negative energy.

Incorporate the exercises in this book into your daily routine.

- Wake up 10 or 15 minutes early every day, go outside, and practice grounding meditation or visualization.
- Before you go to work, practice a protection visualization or meditation to shield yourself from negative energy throughout the day.
- After you get home, perform a body cleansing meditation to release any negativity you may have absorbed.
- Before bed, write in your journal to reflect on your day and practice an energy-resting exercise.

Embrace your empathy and be proud of your unique abilities. Heal yourself from the past and forgive those who hurt you. Protect your energy from negative people and use your gift to make the world a better place.

Conclusion

Empathy is a gift that should be nourished and embraced. It gives you unique abilities that allow you to understand others on a deeper level, feel their pain, and relate to their struggles. Your family and friends love talking to you about their problems. You not only understand them, but you can also sense all the thoughts and emotions they hide. While many people wish they had your gift, you often feel like it is a curse. Your sensitivity to negative energy and constantly feeling drained and exhausted can make you hate your empathy.

However, various techniques can protect your energy from toxic people, energy vampires, and feeling depleted. The book began by explaining empathy from spiritual and scientific aspects. It also explored the advantages and disadvantages of being an empath.

Many confuse *empathy* and *high sensitivity*. However, these are two different terms. Understanding the difference will help you when setting boundaries and managing your energy.

Protecting your energy requires you to understand how it functions. You learned about energy anatomy and the four main subtle bodies. You also put what you have learned into practice with various techniques and strategies. The book provided grounding, breathwork, meditation, and visualization techniques that can help balance and strengthen your energy.

Toxic individuals and unhealthy relationships can impact your energy field. When you are around these people, you absorb their negative energy and intentions, leaving you emotionally drained. Recognizing their pattern of behavior is necessary to protect your energy when interacting with them.

Some places can even carry residual negative energy that only an empath can sense. These environments can make you feel physically and emotionally drained.

Energy vampires and manipulators take advantage of the empaths' good nature. Their constant complaints, negativity, and manipulation can drain your energy and make you exhausted.

You need to release the negative energy you absorb from these individuals and set boundaries to protect yourself in the future. However, some energies become attached to you, leaving you energetically hollow. Meditation, breathwork, and other exercises can help you detach from these energies.

Empaths should take time to recharge and heal after spending time with toxic individuals. Various energy healing practices can be incorporated into your daily routine to restore balance and boost your mental and emotional well-being.

Embrace your empathic gifts and release doubts, fears, and mental limitations that hold you back.

Your journey doesn't end when you finish this book. You should continue learning and exploring your empathic abilities. Practice the exercises in the book daily to heal and protect your energy.

If you enjoyed this book, I'd greatly appreciate a review on Amazon because it helps me to create more books that people want. It would mean a lot to hear from you.

To leave a review:
1. Open your camera app.
2. Point your mobile device at the QR code.
3. The review page will appear in your web browser.

Thanks for your support!

Here's another book by Mari Silva that you might like

Your Free Gift
(only available for a limited time)

Thanks for getting this book! If you want to learn more about various spirituality topics, then join Mari Silva's community and get a free guided meditation MP3 for awakening your third eye. This guided meditation mp3 is designed to open and strengthen ones third eye so you can experience a higher state of consciousness. Simply visit the link below the image to get started.

https://spiritualityspot.com/meditation

Or, Scan the QR code!

References

Chen, L. (2024, August 16). Lisa Chen Therapy Blog. Lisa Chen & Associates Therapy; Lisa Chen Therapy. https://www.lisachentherapy.com/blog/are-you-an-hsp-empath-or-both

Cleveland Clinic. (2023, January 20). What Is a Highly Sensitive Person (HSP)? Cleveland Clinic. https://health.clevelandclinic.org/highly-sensitive-person

Orloff, J. (2020, November 19). The Top 10 Traits of an Empath. Judith Orloff MD. https://drjudithorloff.com/top-10-traits-of-an-empath/

Psychological & Educational Consulting. (2019, January 11). The Difference Between Highly Sensitive People and Empaths. Psychological and Educational Consulting. https://www.psychedconsult.com/the-difference-between-highly-sensitive-people-and-empaths/

Psychology Today Staff. (2025). Highly Sensitive Person | Psychology Today. Www.psychologytoday.com. https://www.psychologytoday.com/us/basics/highly-sensitive-person

Tabak, J. (2021, July 6). My Experience as a Highly Sensitive Person - Empathy for Change - Medium. Medium; Empathy for Change. https://medium.com/empathy-for-change/my-experience-as-a-highly-sensitive-person-eb34d9b076da

View. (2016, January 28). Up and Down The Empathy Spectrum. UnPickled. https://unpickledblog.com/2016/01/27/up-and-down-the-empathy-spectrum/

Voices of Academia. (2022, December 2). From Kryptonite to Superpower: My Story of Being an Empath in Academia by Claudia Mirretta Barone. Voices of Academia. https://voicesofacademia.com/2022/12/02/from-kryptonite-to-superpower-my-story-of-being-an-empath-in-academia-by-claudia-mirretta-barone/

7 Ways To Reset Your Energy & Cleanse Your Aura When You Feel Blocked. (2022, September 21). Mindbodygreen. https://www.mindbodygreen.com/articles/aura-cleansing

gatewayofhealing. (2024, September 5). 6 Signs You Have Low Aura & 10 Tips To Improve - Energy Healing | Healer in Gurgaon. Energy Healing | Healer in Gurgaon. https://www.gatewayofhealing.com/6-signs-you-have-low-aura-10-tips-to-improve/

Stelter, G. (2016, October 4). A Beginner's Guide to the 7 Chakras and Their Meanings. Healthline; Healthline Media. https://www.healthline.com/health/fitness-exercise/7-chakras

Summer, I. (2023, September 28). Energy Anatomy: Exploring the Subtle Bodies and Auras. Medium; Medium. https://medium.com/@indigo.summer444/energy-anatomy-exploring-the-subtle-bodies-and-auras-5bedda73849c

Thriving As An Empath: A Primer For Energy Maintenance | The Vital Spirit. (2016, October 26). The Vital Spirit. https://thevitalspirit.net/2016/10/25/thriving-as-an-empath-a-primer-for-energy-maintenance/

B, R. (2016, December 20). Spirit & Muse. Spirit & Muse. https://www.spiritandmuse.com/spirit-muse-blog/a-10-minute-technique-for-clearing-your-energy-field

Be Earth. (2024). Chakra Balancing: 6 Benefits of Aligning the Seven Chakras | Be Earth | Blog. Be Earth Yoga. https://www.beearth.com.hk/blog/Chakra_Balancing:_6_Benefits_of_Aligning_the_Seven_Chakras

Bjelland, J. (2022, December 5). Julie Bjelland. Julie Bjelland. https://www.juliebjelland.com/hsp-blog/protecting-and-clearing-your-energy

Body Scan Meditation (Greater Good in Action). (n.d.). Ggia.berkeley.edu. https://ggia.berkeley.edu/practice/body_scan_meditation

Bonnard, P. (2023, October 31). A Clearing Energy Meditation You Can Practice In 5 Minutes Or Less. Starchaser-Healing Arts. https://www.starchaser-healingarts.com/a-clearing-energy-meditation-you-can-practice-in-5-minutes-or-less/

Calm. (2023, October 16). Box breathing: how to do it and why it matters (C. Mosunic, Ed.). Calm Blog. https://www.calm.com/blog/box-breathing

Connect, S. (2024). Muladhara Chakra: Grounding Energy for Strength and Stability. Sattvaconnect.com. https://sattvaconnect.com/blog/muladhara-chakra-grounding-energy-strength-stability

Department of Health & Human Services. (2015, September 30). Breathing to reduce stress. Www.betterhealth.vic.gov.au. https://www.betterhealth.vic.gov.au/health/healthyliving/breathing-to-reduce-stress

Fischer, K. (2024, May 3). Grounding: Techniques and benefits. WebMD. https://www.webmd.com/balance/grounding-benefits

G, R. (2019). A Visualisation to Create A Protective Shield or Bubble. Rachelgtherapy.co.uk. https://www.rachelgtherapy.co.uk/create-a-protective-shield

Harwood, R. (2024, November 30). The Power of Intention and Visualization in Energy Healing. Challenge to Change. https://www.challengetochangeinc.com/post/the-power-of-intention-and-visualization-in-energy-healing?srsltid=AfmBOoqd7us2NDfOpTrhWfozpCKnw1i1VBG0psJETBQF5tK6qOeNGm4K

Higher Self Yoga Editors. (2024). 10 Ways to Connect With Your Higher Self. Higherselfyoga.org. https://www.higherselfyoga.org/articles/10-ways-to-connect-with-your-higher-self

in. (2023, February 21). Shape Your Vibe. Shape Your Vibe. https://www.shapeyourvibe.com/blog-holistic-health-self-healing/breathwork-left-vs-right-nostril

Loose, M. (2024, July 4). A Meditation to Connect with Your Higher Self. TUT. https://www.tut.com/a-meditation-to-connect-with-your-higher-self/

MacIntyre, B. (2020, July 9). How to Feel More Balanced as an Energy Sensitive Soul. Brenda MacIntyre, Medicine Song Woman. https://medicinesongwoman.com/how-to-feel-more-balanced-as-an-energy-sensitive-soul

Nash, J. (2022, June 19). How to Practice Visualization Meditation: 3 Best Scripts. PositivePsychology.com. https://positivepsychology.com/visualization-meditation/

Orloff, J. (2018). 5 Protection Techniques for Sensitive People. Psychology Today. https://www.psychologytoday.com/us/blog/the-empaths-survival-guide/201804/5-protection-techniques-for-sensitive-people

Othership, & reserved, A. right. (2021, October 17). Breathwork For Energy: 3 Ways It Can Enhance Your Life. Www.othership.us. https://www.othership.us/resources/breathwork-for-energy

Paul, J. (2023, September 28). How to Visualize and Manifest: Creating Positive Energy in 5 Simple Steps - Dr. Magie Cook | Motivational Latina Speaker | LGBTQ. Dr. Magie Cook | Motivational Latina Speaker | LGBTQ. https://magiecook.com/blog/how-to-visualize-and-manifest-creating-positive-energy-in-5-simple-steps/

Prashant Jakhmola, A. (2024). Yoga Teacher Training in Rishikesh - Yoga School Rishikesh. Yogavidyaschool.com.

https://www.yogavidyaschool.com/blog/chakras-advanced-meditation-techniques-for-your-energy-flow

Burney, D. (2009). Spiritual Clearings. North Atlantic Books.

Campion, L. (2021). Energy Healing for Empaths. New Harbinger Publications.

Carruthers, A. (2013). Freedom from toxic relationships: Moving on from the family, work, and relationship issues that bring you down. Tarcher/Penguin.

Chapman, G., & White, P. (2014). Rising Above a Toxic Workplace. Moody Publishers.

Dykas, E. M. (2021). Toxic Relationships. P & R Publishing Co (Pres).

Edwards, S. K. (2018). Smudging: Clear negative energy from your home & life. Wildhair Studios, Llc.

Fontana, D. (2012). Creative Meditation & Visualisation. Watkins Media Limited.

Grace, A. (2021). Protect Your Energy. Ascending Vibrations.

Gregory, L. (2016). Difficult people: Strategies for dealing with toxic people. Luke F. Gregory.

Hall, J. (2020). Crystals for energy protection. Hay House UK.

Northrup, M. D., Christiane. (2018). Dodging Energy Vampires. Hay House.

O'Connor, D. (2011). Energy Vampire Slaying 101: How to combat and defeat toxic attitudes and negative behavior in your office, your home, and yourself. Createspace.

Orloff, J. (2017). The Empath's Survival Guide. Sounds True.

Orloff, J. (2019). Thriving as an empath : a daily guide to empower sensitive people. Sounds True.

Ornelas, S. (2007). Energy Vampires: Managing Stress & Negative Thoughts in your Personal & Professional Life. Lulu.com.

Reichter, S. (2018). Spiritual Protection. Red Wheel/Weiser.

White, A., & James, R. (2021). Empath. Alakai Publishing LLC.

Xavier, N. S. (2006). Fulfilling Heart and Soul. AuthorHouse.

Balance, T. M. (2024, December 17). Empaths and Energy Drain: How to Set Boundaries and Protect Your Power. The Mindful Balance. https://www.themindfulbalancetoolkit.blog/post/empaths-and-energy-drain-how-to-set-boundaries-and-protect-your-power

Burns, C. L. (2016, October 26). Why Attachment Styles Can Make or Break Your Success in Love. Acing Life. https://acinglife.com/why-attachment-styles-can-make-or-break-your-success-in-love/

Calm. (2024, January 12). Calm Blog (C. Mosunic, Ed.). Calm Blog. https://www.calm.com/blog/energy-vampire

Caudle, N. (2023, January 28). Overcoming Generational Trauma and Closing Karmic Family Cycles. Medium. https://medium.com/@nicole.bcaudle/overcoming-generational-trauma-and-closing-karmic-family-cycles-7ffc4c23caf

d'Arcanum, S. (2023, September 24). Truth Resonates. Truth Resonates. https://www.truthresonates.com/writings/clarity-around-karma

Dey, M. (2024, April 7). Letting Go: How to Achieve Inner Peace through Detachment. Create a Great Life. https://meerabelledey.com/cultivate-detachment-for-inner-peace/

Erica. (2020, November 23). Soul Dreams Studio. Soul Dreams Studio. https://souldreamsstudio.com/soulblog/2020/11/23/2020-11-22-what-are-energy-cords

Gillette, H. (2013, November 14). Energy Vampire: Signs, Causes, and How to Protect Your Energy. Psych Central. https://psychcentral.com/blog/how-to-avoid-being-drained-by-energy-vampires#how-to-protect-yourself

Goddess, M. (2024, April 4). Energy Imprint, Energy Cord, Or Entity Attachment? Psychic Bloggers. https://psychicbloggers.com/archives/8322

Harrison, P. (2020, December 8). Guided Meditation For Letting Go With Script. THE DAILY MEDITATION. https://www.thedailymeditation.com/meditation-script-for-letting-go

Health, M. (2023). Understanding Pathological Emotional Attachment: Causes, Symptoms, and Treatment. The Kusnacht Practice. https://kusnachtpractice.com/articles/understanding-pathological-emotional-attachment-causes-symptoms-and-treatment/

Holland, K. (2018, February 13). How to Recognize and Respond to Energy Vampires at Home, Work, and More. Healthline; Healthline Media. https://www.healthline.com/health/mental-health/energy-vampires#takeaway

Huntington, C. (2017). Emotional Attachment: Meaning, Problems, & Signs. The Berkeley Well-Being Institute. https://www.berkeleywellbeing.com/emotional-attachment.html

Innerfire. (2023, December 11). Three breathing exercises to boost your energy. Wimhofmethod.com; Wim hof Method. https://www.wimhofmethod.com/blog/three-breathing-exercises-to-boost-your-energy

Are Empaths Born or Made? (n.d.). Embodied Wellness, PLLC. https://www.embodiedwellnesstherapy.com/blog/are-empaths-born-or-made

Ayoola, E. (2023). 5 Steps That Helped Me Learn To Forgive My Parents. Parents. https://www.parents.com/five-steps-that-helped-me-learn-to-forgive-my-parents-7092997

Baulch, D. J. (2023, October 24). What is Inner Child Work and How Do You Get Started. Inner Melbourne Psychology. https://www.innermelbpsychology.com.au/what-is-inner-child-work-and-how-to-get-started/

Cooks-Campbell, A. (2022, March 15). How inner child work enables healing and playful discovery. BetterUp. https://www.betterup.com/blog/inner-child-work

Cutting Energy Cords For Personal Growth. (2019, September 23). Insight Timer Blog. https://insighttimer.com/blog/cutting-energy-cords/

Gomes, A. (2024, April 12). 100 Positive Affirmations For Empaths: Boost Resilience. The Good Positive. https://thegoodpositive.com/positive-affirmations-for-empaths/

How To Do Low Lunge For Beginners - Body By Yoga. (2021, February 13). Bodybyyoga. Training. https://bodybyyoga.training/yoga-for-beginners/pose-guides/how-to-do-low-lunge-for-beginners/

How to set personal boundaries to protect your energy. (n.d.). Groov | Workplace Mental Wellbeing Platform. https://www.groovnow.com/blog/how-to-set-personal-boundaries-to-protect-your-energy

Insight Network, Inc. (2025a). Insight Timer - #1 Free Meditation App for Sleep, Relax & More. Insighttimer.com. https://insighttimer.com/meditation-courses/10-tools-for-empaths-turning-sensitivity-into-the-gift-of-selflove

Insight Network, Inc. (2025b). Insight Timer - #1 Free Meditation App for Sleep, Relax & More. Insighttimer.com. https://insighttimer.com/abrighterwild/guided-meditations/energy-shielding-meditation-2

Li, X., Zhou, L., Ding, C., & Li, Z. (2024). Effects of childhood emotional neglect on pain empathy: Evidence from event-related potentials. Children and Youth Services Review, 160, 107534–107534. https://doi.org/10.1016/j.childyouth.2024.107534

New Horizon. (n.d.). Connect to your Higher Self. Insighttimer.com. https://insighttimer.com/newhorizon/guided-meditations/connect-to-your-higher-self

O'Connell, R. (2023, June 1). The Importance of Overcoming Limiting Beliefs (With Examples) | Guider AI. Guider-Ai.com. https://guider-ai.com/blog/overcoming-limiting-beliefs/

O'Neill, H. (2022, October 18). Suburban Witchery. Suburban Witchery. https://www.suburbanwitchery.com/blog/cord-cutting?srsltid=AfmBOopnjsLCDkKqYmYFFSm3SfjXwIVHnby2M3wV3Dlp9K9gT4JvVMuE

Owner. (2024, July 2). 4 Limiting Beliefs Preventing You from Leading with Empathy - Teach Empowered. Teach Empowered.

https://teachempowered.com/4-limiting-beliefs-preventing-you-from-leading-with-empathy/

Pizer, A. (2023, July 31). 5 Pranayama Breathing Exercises for Yoga Beginners. Liforme. https://liforme.com/blogs/blog/5-pranayama-breathing-exercises-for-yoga-beginners

Reid, S. (2022, May 3). Empathy: How to Feel and Respond to the Emotions of Others. HelpGuide.org.
https://www.helpguide.org/relationships/communication/empathy

Sobel, A. (2016, January 27). Eight Ways to Improve Your Empathy. Andrew Sobel. https://andrewsobel.com/article/eight-ways-to-improve-your-empathy/

Speaks, V. (2023, May 19). 4 ways I learned to transmute energy - Veneka Speaks - Medium. Medium. https://medium.com/@veneka/4-ways-i-learned-to-transmute-energy-9725424a59f

Sutton, J. (2020, July 15). Mindful Walking & Walking Meditation: A Restorative Practice. PositivePsychology.com. https://positivepsychology.com/mindful-walking/#practice

Suwal, C. (2020, July 21). What Happens When You Open Your Third Eye. Insight Timer Blog. https://insighttimer.com/blog/what-happens-when-you-open-your-third-eye/

Team Luke. (2024, August 16). Be Happy: 10 Free Ways To Raise Your Vibration RIGHT NOW. Luke Coutinho.
https://www.lukecoutinho.com/blogs/emotional-wellness/feel-happy-raise-vibration/

Villines, Z. (2023, August 29). Empaths and anxiety: Link, causes, and coping. Www.medicalnewstoday.com.
https://www.medicalnewstoday.com/articles/empaths-and-anxiety

YINA BEAUTÉ. (2024, November 8). Shaking Qigong. YINA.
https://yina.co/blogs/wellness-guide/shaking-qigong

7 Ways To Reset Your Energy & Cleanse Your Aura When You Feel Blocked. (2022, September 21). Mindbodygreen.
https://www.mindbodygreen.com/articles/aura-cleansing

Are Empaths Born or Made? (n.d.). Embodied Wellness, PLLC.
https://www.embodiedwellnesstherapy.com/blog/are-empaths-born-or-made

Ayoola, E. (2023). 5 Steps That Helped Me Learn To Forgive My Parents. Parents. https://www.parents.com/five-steps-that-helped-me-learn-to-forgive-my-parents-7092997

B, R. (2016, December 20). Spirit & Muse. Spirit & Muse.
https://www.spiritandmuse.com/spirit-muse-blog/a-10-minute-technique-for-clearing-your-energy-field

Balance, T. M. (2024, December 17). Empaths and Energy Drain: How to Set Boundaries and Protect Your Power. The Mindful Balance. https://www.themindfulbalancetoolkit.blog/post/empaths-and-energy-drain-how-to-set-boundaries-and-protect-your-power

Baulch, D. J. (2023, October 24). What is Inner Child Work and How Do You Get Started. Inner Melbourne Psychology. https://www.innermelbpsychology.com.au/what-is-inner-child-work-and-how-to-get-started/

Be Earth. (2024). Chakra Balancing: 6 Benefits of Aligning the Seven Chakras | Be Earth | Blog. Be Earth Yoga. https://www.beearth.com.hk/blog/Chakra_Balancing:_6_Benefits_of_Aligning_the_Seven_Chakras

Bjelland, J. (2022, December 5). Julie Bjelland. Julie Bjelland. https://www.juliebjelland.com/hsp-blog/protecting-and-clearing-your-energy

Body Scan Meditation (Greater Good in Action). (n.d.). Ggia.berkeley.edu. https://ggia.berkeley.edu/practice/body_scan_meditation

Bonnard, P. (2023, October 31). A Clearing Energy Meditation You Can Practice In 5 Minutes Or Less. Starchaser-Healing Arts. https://www.starchaser-healingarts.com/a-clearing-energy-meditation-you-can-practice-in-5-minutes-or-less/

Burney, D. (2009). Spiritual Clearings. North Atlantic Books.

Burns, C. L. (2016, October 26). Why Attachment Styles Can Make or Break Your Success in Love. Acing Life. https://acinglife.com/why-attachment-styles-can-make-or-break-your-success-in-love/

Calm. (2023, October 16). Box breathing: how to do it and why it matters (C. Mosunic, Ed.). Calm Blog. https://www.calm.com/blog/box-breathing

Calm. (2024, January 12). Calm Blog (C. Mosunic, Ed.). Calm Blog. https://www.calm.com/blog/energy-vampire

Campion, L. (2021). Energy Healing for Empaths. New Harbinger Publications.

Carruthers, A. (2013). Freedom from toxic relationships: Moving on from the family, work, and relationship issues that bring you down. Tarcher/Penguin.

Caudle, N. (2023, January 28). Overcoming Generational Trauma and Closing Karmic Family Cycles. Medium. https://medium.com/@nicole.bcaudle/overcoming-generational-trauma-and-closing-karmic-family-cycles-7ffc4c23caf

Chapman, G., & White, P. (2014). Rising Above a Toxic Workplace. Moody Publishers.

Chen, L. (2024, August 16). Lisa Chen Therapy Blog. Lisa Chen & Associates Therapy; Lisa Chen Therapy. https://www.lisachentherapy.com/blog/are-you-an-hsp-empath-or-both

Cleveland Clinic. (2023, January 20). What Is a Highly Sensitive Person (HSP)? Cleveland Clinic. https://health.clevelandclinic.org/highly-sensitive-person

Connect, S. (2024). Muladhara Chakra: Grounding Energy for Strength and Stability. Sattvaconnect.com. https://sattvaconnect.com/blog/muladhara-chakra-grounding-energy-strength-stability

Cooks-Campbell, A. (2022, March 15). How inner child work enables healing and playful discovery. BetterUp. https://www.betterup.com/blog/inner-child-work

Cutting Energy Cords For Personal Growth. (2019, September 23). Insight Timer Blog. https://insighttimer.com/blog/cutting-energy-cords/

d'Arcanum, S. (2023, September 24). Truth Resonates. Truth Resonates. https://www.truthresonates.com/writings/clarity-around-karma

Department of Health & Human Services. (2015, September 30). Breathing to reduce stress. Www.betterhealth.vic.gov.au. https://www.betterhealth.vic.gov.au/health/healthyliving/breathing-to-reduce-stress

Dey, M. (2024, April 7). Letting Go: How to Achieve Inner Peace through Detachment. Create a Great Life. https://meerabelledey.com/cultivate-detachment-for-inner-peace/

Dykas, E. M. (2021). Toxic Relationships. P & R Publishing Co (Pres).

Edwards, S. K. (2018). Smudging: Clear negative energy from your home & life. Wildhair Studios, Llc.

Erica. (2020, November 23). Soul Dreams Studio. Soul Dreams Studio. https://souldreamsstudio.com/soulblog/2020/11/23/2020-11-22-what-are-energy-cords

Fischer, K. (2024, May 3). Grounding: Techniques and benefits. WebMD. https://www.webmd.com/balance/grounding-benefits

Fontana, D. (2012). Creative Meditation & Visualisation. Watkins Media Limited.

G, R. (2019). A Visualisation to Create A Protective Shield or Bubble. Rachelgtherapy.co.uk. https://www.rachelgtherapy.co.uk/create-a-protective-shield

gatewayofhealing. (2024, September 5). 6 Signs You Have Low Aura & 10 Tips To Improve - Energy Healing | Healer in Gurgaon. Energy Healing | Healer in Gurgaon. https://www.gatewayofhealing.com/6-signs-you-have-low-aura-10-tips-to-improve/

Gillette, H. (2013, November 14). Energy Vampire: Signs, Causes, and How to Protect Your Energy. Psych Central. https://psychcentral.com/blog/how-to-avoid-being-drained-by-energy-vampires#how-to-protect-yourself

Goddess, M. (2024, April 4). Energy Imprint, Energy Cord, Or Entity Attachment? Psychic Bloggers. https://psychicbloggers.com/archives/8322

Gomes, A. (2024, April 12). 100 Positive Affirmations For Empaths: Boost Resilience. The Good Positive. https://thegoodpositive.com/positive-affirmations-for-empaths/

Grace, A. (2021). Protect Your Energy. Ascending Vibrations.

Gregory, L. (2016). Difficult people: Strategies for dealing with toxic people. Luke F. Gregory.

Hall, J. (2020). Crystals for energy protection. Hay House UkUK.

Harrison, P. (2020, December 8). Guided Meditation For Letting Go With Script. THE DAILY MEDITATION. https://www.thedailymeditation.com/meditation-script-for-letting-go

Harwood, R. (2024, November 30). The Power of Intention and Visualization in Energy Healing. Challenge to Change. https://www.challengetochangeinc.com/post/the-power-of-intention-and-visualization-in-energy-healing?srsltid=AfmBOoqd7us2NDfOpTrhWfozpCKnw1i1VBG0psJETBQF5tK6qOeNGm4K

Health, M. (2023). Understanding Pathological Emotional Attachment: Causes, Symptoms, and Treatment. The Kusnacht Practice. https://kusnachtpractice.com/articles/understanding-pathological-emotional-attachment-causes-symptoms-and-treatment/

Higher Self Yoga Editors. (2024). 10 Ways to Connect With Your Higher Self. Higherselfyoga.org. https://www.higherselfyoga.org/articles/10-ways-to-connect-with-your-higher-self

Holland, K. (2018, February 13). How to Recognize and Respond to Energy Vampires at Home, Work, and More. Healthline; Healthline Media. https://www.healthline.com/health/mental-health/energy-vampires#takeaway

How To Do Low Lunge For Beginners - Body By Yoga. (2021, February 13). Bodybyyoga. Training. https://bodybyyoga.training/yoga-for-beginners/pose-guides/how-to-do-low-lunge-for-beginners/

How to set personal boundaries to protect your energy. (n.d.). Groov | Workplace Mental Wellbeing Platform. https://www.groovnow.com/blog/how-to-set-personal-boundaries-to-protect-your-energy

Huntington, C. (2017). Emotional Attachment: Meaning, Problems, & Signs. The Berkeley Well-Being Institute. https://www.berkeleywellbeing.com/emotional-attachment.html

in. (2023, February 21). Shape Your Vibe. Shape Your Vibe. https://www.shapeyourvibe.com/blog-holistic-health-self-healing/breathwork-left-vs-right-nostril

Innerfire. (2023, December 11). Three breathing exercises to boost your energy. Wimhofmethod.com; Wim hof Method.

https://www.wimhofmethod.com/blog/three-breathing-exercises-to-boost-your-energy

Insight Network, Inc. (2025a). Insight Timer - #1 Free Meditation App for Sleep, Relax & More. Insighttimer.com. https://insighttimer.com/meditation-courses/10-tools-for-empaths-turning-sensitivity-into-the-gift-of-selflove

Insight Network, Inc. (2025b). Insight Timer - #1 Free Meditation App for Sleep, Relax & More. Insighttimer.com. https://insighttimer.com/abrighterwild/guided-meditations/energy-shielding-meditation-2

Li, X., Zhou, L., Ding, C., & Li, Z. (2024). Effects of childhood emotional neglect on pain empathy: Evidence from event-related potentials. Children and Youth Services Review, 160, 107534-107534. https://doi.org/10.1016/j.childyouth.2024.107534

Loose, M. (2024, July 4). A Meditation to Connect with Your Higher Self. TUT. https://www.tut.com/a-meditation-to-connect-with-your-higher-self/

MacIntyre, B. (2020, July 9). How to Feel More Balanced as an Energy Sensitive Soul. Brenda MacIntyre, Medicine Song Woman. https://medicinesongwoman.com/how-to-feel-more-balanced-as-an-energy-sensitive-soul

Nash, J. (2022, June 19). How to Practice Visualization Meditation: 3 Best Scripts. PositivePsychology.com. https://positivepsychology.com/visualization-meditation/

New Horizon. (n.d.). Connect to your Higher Self. Insighttimer.com. https://insighttimer.com/newhorizon/guided-meditations/connect-to-your-higher-self

Northrup, M. D., Christiane. (2018). Dodging Energy Vampires. Hay House.

O'Connell, R. (2023, June 1). The Importance of Overcoming Limiting Beliefs (With Examples) | Guider AI. Guider-Ai.com. https://guider-ai.com/blog/overcoming-limiting-beliefs/

O'Connor, D. (2011). Energy Vampire Slaying 101: How to combat and defeat toxic attitudes and negative behavior in your office, your home, and yourself. Createspace.

O'Neill, H. (2022, October 18). Suburban Witchery. Suburban Witchery. https://www.suburbanwitchery.com/blog/cord-cutting?srsltid=AfmBOopnjsLCDkKqYmYFFSm3SfjXwIVHnby2M3wV3Dlp9K9gT4JvVMuE

Orloff, J. (2017). The Empath's Survival Guide. Sounds True.

Orloff, J. (2018). 5 Protection Techniques for Sensitive People. Psychology Today. https://www.psychologytoday.com/us/blog/the-empaths-survival-guide/201804/5-protection-techniques-for-sensitive-people

Orloff, J. (2019). Thriving as an empath: a daily guide to empower sensitive people. Sounds True.

Orloff, J. (2020, November 19). The Top 10 Traits of an Empath. Judith Orloff MD. https://drjudithorloff.com/top-10-traits-of-an-empath/

Ornelas, S. (2007). Energy Vampires: Managing Stress & Negative Thoughts in your Personal & Professional Life. Lulu.com.

Othership, & reserved, A. right. (2021, October 17). Breathwork For Energy: 3 Ways It Can Enhance Your Life. Www.othership.us. https://www.othership.us/resources/breathwork-for-energy

Owner. (2024, July 2). 4 Limiting Beliefs Preventing You from Leading with Empathy - Teach Empowered. Teach Empowered. https://teachempowered.com/4-limiting-beliefs-preventing-you-from-leading-with-empathy/

Paul, J. (2023, September 28). How to Visualize and Manifest: Creating Positive Energy in 5 Simple Steps - Dr. Magie Cook | Motivational Latina Speaker | LGBTQ. Dr. Magie Cook | Motivational Latina Speaker | LGBTQ. https://magiecook.com/blog/how-to-visualize-and-manifest-creating-positive-energy-in-5-simple-steps/

Pizer, A. (2023, July 31). 5 Pranayama Breathing Exercises for Yoga Beginners. Liforme. https://liforme.com/blogs/blog/5-pranayama-breathing-exercises-for-yoga-beginners

Prashant Jakhmola, A. (2024). Yoga Teacher Training in Rishikesh - Yoga School Rishikesh. Yogavidyaschool.com. https://www.yogavidyaschool.com/blog/chakras-advanced-meditation-techniques-for-your-energy-flow

Psychological & Educational Consulting. (2019, January 11). The Difference Between Highly Sensitive People and Empaths. Psychological and Educational Consulting. https://www.psychedconsult.com/the-difference-between-highly-sensitive-people-and-empaths/

Psychology Today Staff. (2025). Highly Sensitive Person | Psychology Today. Www.psychologytoday.com. https://www.psychologytoday.com/us/basics/highly-sensitive-person

Reichter, S. (2018). Spiritual Protection. Red Wheel/Weiser.

Reid, S. (2022, May 3). Empathy: How to Feel and Respond to the Emotions of Others. HelpGuide.org. https://www.helpguide.org/relationships/communication/empathy

Sobel, A. (2016, January 27). Eight Ways to Improve Your Empathy. Andrew Sobel. https://andrewsobel.com/article/eight-ways-to-improve-your-empathy/

Speaks, V. (2023, May 19). 4 ways I learned to transmute energy - Veneka Speaks - Medium. Medium. https://medium.com/@veneka/4-ways-i-learned-to-transmute-energy-9725424a59f

Stelter, G. (2016, October 4). A Beginner's Guide to the 7 Chakras and Their Meanings. Healthline; Healthline Media. https://www.healthline.com/health/fitness-exercise/7-chakras

Summer, I. (2023, September 28). Energy Anatomy: Exploring the Subtle Bodies and Auras. Medium; Medium. https://medium.com/@indigo.summer444/energy-anatomy-exploring-the-subtle-bodies-and-auras-5bedda73849c

Sutton, J. (2020, July 15). Mindful Walking & Walking Meditation: A Restorative Practice. PositivePsychology.com. https://positivepsychology.com/mindful-walking/#practice

Suwal, C. (2020, July 21). What Happens When You Open Your Third Eye. Insight Timer Blog. https://insighttimer.com/blog/what-happens-when-you-open-your-third-eye/

Tabak, J. (2021, July 6). My Experience as a Highly Sensitive Person - Empathy for Change - Medium. Medium; Empathy for Change. https://medium.com/empathy-for-change/my-experience-as-a-highly-sensitive-person-eb34d9b076da

Team Luke. (2024, August 16). Be Happy: 10 Free Ways To Raise Your Vibration RIGHT NOW. Luke Coutinho. https://www.lukecoutinho.com/blogs/emotional-wellness/feel-happy-raise-vibration/

Thriving As An Empath: A Primer For Energy Maintenance | The Vital Spirit. (2016, October 26). The Vital Spirit. https://thevitalspirit.net/2016/10/25/thriving-as-an-empath-a-primer-for-energy-maintenance/

View. (2016, January 28). Up and Down The Empathy Spectrum. UnPickled. https://unpickledblog.com/2016/01/27/up-and-down-the-empathy-spectrum/

Villines, Z. (2023, August 29). Empaths and anxiety: Link, causes, and coping. Www.medicalnewstoday.com. https://www.medicalnewstoday.com/articles/empaths-and-anxiety

Voices of Academia. (2022, December 2). From Kryptonite to Superpower: My Story of Being an Empath in Academia by Claudia Mirretta Barone. Voices of Academia. https://voicesofacademia.com/2022/12/02/from-kryptonite-to-superpower-my-story-of-being-an-empath-in-academia-by-claudia-mirretta-barone/

White, A., & James, R. (2021). Empath. Alakai Publishing LLC.

Xavier, N. S. (2006). Fulfilling Heart and Soul. AuthorHouse.

YINA BEAUTÉ. (2024, November 8). Shaking Qigong. YINA. https://yina.co/blogs/wellness-guide/shaking-qigong

Image Sources

1. Photo by Anna Shvets: https://www.pexels.com/photo/woman-comforting-friend-3727564/
2. Photo by Anna Shvets: https://www.pexels.com/photo/close-up-shot-of-mri-results-4226264/
3. Photo by Sora Shimazaki: https://www.pexels.com/photo/woman-suffering-from-a-stomach-pain-5938358/
4. Photo by Mikhail Nilov: https://www.pexels.com/photo/woman-in-red-dress-holding-fire-6931866/
5. RootOfAllLight, CC BY-SA 4.0 <https://creativecommons.org/licenses/by-sa/4.0>, via Wikimedia Commons https://commons.wikimedia.org/wiki/File:7ChakrasFemale.png
6. Suganya, Kanmani, and Byung-Soo Koo, CC BY 4.0 <https://creativecommons.org/licenses/by/4.0>, via Wikimedia Commons https://commons.wikimedia.org/wiki/File:Gut-Brain_Axis.png
7. Photo by Emiliano Vittoriosi on Unsplash https://unsplash.com/photos/woman-with-piercing-on-nose-o37-NDE2AHk
8. Photo by RUPAM DUTTA on Unsplash https://unsplash.com/photos/man-in-green-and-black-plaid-dress-shirt-wearing-black-and-white-headphones-5OMff2RDqPs
9. Photo by Elena Espejel on Unsplash https://unsplash.com/photos/a-close-up-of-a-person-with-a-sunflower-drx4q77KH3Y
10. Photo by Etienne Boulanger on Unsplash https://unsplash.com/photos/silhouette-of-man-and-woman-sitting-on-ottoman-erCPgyXNlto
11. Photo by Los Muertos Crew: https://www.pexels.com/photo/woman-lying-by-mortar-8391652/

12 IXSUN, CC BY-SA 4.0 <https://creativecommons.org/licenses/by-sa/4.0>, via Wikimedia Commons https://commons.wikimedia.org/wiki/File: Chakras_en_en_el_cuerpo_humano.jpeg

13 Photo by Roberto Nickson on Unsplash https://unsplash.com/photos/woman-in-white-bathtub-holding-clear-drinking-glass-YCW4BEhKluw

14 Photo by THLT LCX on Unsplash https://unsplash.com/photos/woman-in-brown-knit-sweater-holding-brown-ceramic-cup-VsI_74zRzAo

15 Photo by Sasan on Unsplash https://unsplash.com/photos/people-walking-on-pathway-between-green-trees-during-daytime-89e0z6zqkAo

16 Photo by Darius Bashar on Unsplash https://unsplash.com/photos/topless-man-wearing-black-beaded-necklace-and-blue-denim-shorts-standing-on-rocky-shore-during-daytime-I8Q261NtB24

17 Photo by RDNE Stock project: https://www.pexels.com/photo/an-elderly-people-standing-while-meditating-at-the-park-8172935/

18 Photo by Yan Krukau: https://www.pexels.com/photo/man-practising-yoga-8436752/

19 Photo by Savanna Goldring: https://www.pexels.com/photo/woman-in-black-sports-bra-and-black-pants-sitting-on-rock-5184327/

20 Photo by Nathan Cowley: https://www.pexels.com/photo/man-in-blue-and-brown-plaid-dress-shirt-touching-his-hair-897817/

21 Photo by Alena Darmel: https://www.pexels.com/photo/a-couple-having-a-conversation-6642995/

22 Photo by Arina Krasnikova: https://www.pexels.com/photo/a-woman-working-from-home-7005399/

23 Photo by Karly Jones on Unsplash https://unsplash.com/photos/white-and-black-textile-on-brown-round-container-4caRljJwGsE

24 Photo by Dan Farrell on Unsplash https://unsplash.com/photos/purple-and-white-heart-shaped-stones-qayNP9ccw9E

25 Photo by BĀBI on Unsplash https://unsplash.com/photos/woman-in-white-tank-top-NW61v3xF0-0

26 Photo by Pixabay: https://www.pexels.com/photo/close-up-photography-of-smartphone-icons-267350/

27 Photo by Kampus Production: https://www.pexels.com/photo/back-view-of-a-person-holding-a-black-picture-frame-8871430/

28 Photo by Photo By: Kaboompics.com: https://www.pexels.com/photo/a-person-holding-a-coloring-pen-6633729/

29 Photo by Arina Krasnikova: https://www.pexels.com/photo/woman-in-white-sweater-and-white-pants-sitting-on-wooden-floor-6998261/

30 Jan Helebrant, CC BY-SA 2.0 <https://creativecommons.org/licenses/by-sa/2.0>, via Wikimedia Commons https://commons.wikimedia.org/wiki/File:Clear_quartz_-_SiO2_(41998339394).jpg

31 Marie-Lan Taÿ Pamart, CC BY 4.0 <https://creativecommons.org/licenses/by/4.0>, via Wikimedia Commons https://commons.wikimedia.org/wiki/File:Amethyst_Siberia_MNHN_Min%C3%A9ralogie.jpg

32 James St. John, CC BY 2.0 <https://creativecommons.org/licenses/by/2.0>, via Wikimedia Commons https://commons.wikimedia.org/wiki/File:Rose_quartz_(32132819430).jpg

33 Rama, CC BY-SA 3.0 FR <https://creativecommons.org/licenses/by-sa/3.0/fr/deed.en>, via Wikimedia Commons https://commons.wikimedia.org/wiki/File:Citrine_quartz-AMGL_79477-P5030194-white.jpg

34 Maatpublishing, CC BY-SA 4.0 <https://creativecommons.org/licenses/by-sa/4.0>, via Wikimedia Commons https://commons.wikimedia.org/wiki/File:Tumbled_carnelian.jpg

35 Jan Helebrant, Attribution-ShareAlike 2.0 Generic, CC BY-SA 2.0, <https://creativecommons.org/licenses/by-sa/2.0/deed.en> https://www.flickr.com/photos/96541566@N06/28838960018

36 Khruner, CC BY-SA 4.0 <https://creativecommons.org/licenses/by-sa/4.0>, via Wikimedia Commons https://commons.wikimedia.org/wiki/File:Mineral_-_Selenite_by_Khruner.png

37 Philippe Giabbanelli, CC BY-SA 3.0 <https://creativecommons.org/licenses/by-sa/3.0>, via Wikimedia Commons https://commons.wikimedia.org/wiki/File:Lapis_Lazulis.jpg

38 あおもりくま、Aomorikuma, CC BY-SA 4.0 <https://creativecommons.org/licenses/by-sa/4.0>, via Wikimedia Commons https://commons.wikimedia.org/wiki/File:Red_Jasper_Tugaru_Nishikiishi_Japan_IMG_8862.jpg

39 Photo by RDNE Stock project: https://www.pexels.com/photo/close-up-shot-of-a-person-doing-an-acupuncture-8313243/

40 Photo by Pixabay: https://www.pexels.com/photo/person-holding-plastic-bottle-260405/

41 Photo by Andrew Neel on Unsplash https://unsplash.com/photos/a-woman-standing-in-a-field-with-her-hair-blowing-in-the-wind-CUBZxkS5ye4

42 Photo by Emma Simpson on Unsplash https://unsplash.com/photos/woman-walking-on-pathway-during-daytime-mNGaaLeWEp0

43 Photo by Marta Wave: https://www.pexels.com/photo/flexible-woman-doing-low-lunge-quad-stretch-6453974/

www.ingramcontent.com/pod-product-compliance
Lightning Source LLC
Chambersburg PA
CBHW051851160426
43209CB00006B/1252